Sabrina Pace-Humphreys is an award-winning business-woman, an ultrarunner, a social justice activist, a mother of four and grandmother of three.

She is co-founder and trustee of the fast-growing community and campaigning charity Black Trail Runners and is also a well-known ultra-marathon runner. She took up running in 2009 as a tool to manage her post-natal depression and, nine years later, completed the 'toughest footrace on earth', a 250km multi-stage ultra-marathon across the Sahara Desert, known as the Marathon des Sables, as the eleventh British woman.

Black Sheep

*A Story of Rural Racism,
Identity and Hope*

Sabrina Pace-Humphreys

QUERCUS

First published in Great Britain in 2023 by

QUERCUS

Quercus Editions Ltd
Carmelite House
50 Victoria Embankment
London EC4Y 0DZ

An Hachette UK company

A CIP catalogue record for this book is available
from the British Library

PB ISBN 978 1 52941 856 9
Ebook ISBN 978 1 52941 857 6

10 9 8 7 6 5 4 3 2 1

Typeset by CC Book Production

Printed and bound in Great Britain by Clays Ltd, Elcograf S.p.A.

Papers used by Quercus are from well-managed forests and other responsible sources.

I dedicate this book to my much-loved late Grandad, my hero, Brian Bernard Brewster.

Grandad, thank you for loving me, protecting me and showing me – through your words and actions – that with you I was safe.

I miss you everyday and I hope I make you proud.

CONTENTS

PROLOGUE: GEORGE FLOYD

THIS TOWN IS RACIST. If you are Black. If you are mixed race.

Look around you. Go to Waitrose, Sainsburys, B&Q. Walk along the canal towpath. You do not see Black people. And if you do, you are shocked. I have been called every name under the sun. If you believe it doesn't happen in this sleepy town then you are deluded.

THIS TOWN IS RACIST. I never thought I would have the courage to say these words out loud. But since I said them – almost shouted them – they have opened up the racist floodgates that lie hidden in the underbelly of this small Cotswold market town. My home town of forty years, and the site of much of the racial trauma I have suffered.

These four words might change the course of my life as I know it.

These four words, together, form a statement of fact, of lived experience, for people of colour living in rural towns across the United Kingdom. For the last forty-two years I have felt unable to say these words because talking about the racism I have experienced, and continue to experience, as a mixed-race person, racialised as Black, means bringing it to the forefront of my mind once again. Talking about it makes me remember the pain, fear and terror of trying to survive living here. Talking about it makes me relive every name I was called, every shove, every traumatic bus journey. Talking about it makes me vulnerable and it gives those kids – who are now adults – permission to hurt me mentally again. And it gives them permission to call me out, to deny they did those things, to paint me as a liar or a drama queen.

I can't ignore, or pretend to ignore, the racism I have experienced at the hands of these white-skinned members of my community, and I can no longer pretend I'm just like them – the people who have never been driven to claw at their skin until it bleeds in order to try and uncover a lighter tone, to make themselves whiter, to fit in.

I'm not like them, and I never have been.

It's June 2020 and a few days ago I witnessed – along with millions of other people around the world – the murder of a Black man called George Floyd. George's murder was captured on a phone screen and streamed across the world. It was one of the most shocking, heart-breaking and utterly devastating pieces of video footage I have ever watched. I can't forget it. I dream about George being murdered, and when I dream it's my face I see, or my son's face, or my grandson's face. I can't stop experiencing a feeling of deep despair, as if someone I know well has been killed. I feel numb, and I don't know what to do with myself.

George was slowly murdered by a police officer who, when he joined the force, swore an oath to protect all members of the American public, no matter what colour or creed. But he didn't protect George. The reason is because George was Black and, in America, as across the world, Black people are treated as inferior to white people. Our lives aren't as important; our skin colour dictates the way in which we are treated physically, mentally and socially.

Black lives don't matter.

But they do.

When in his final moments George called out for his mama, a box inside me that I've kept locked and triple-bolted burst open, never to be closed again. The opening of this, my Pandora's box, manifested in uncontrollable sobs but, as I now know, it heralded something much more profound and life-changing.

I can't breathe.

George's words made me come to this, my first ever protest, this town's first ever Black Lives Matter protest. I wasn't going to come, because what difference will it make? It won't bring George back, will it? It won't erase years of persecution of

Black people. This tiny little market town in the Cotswolds can't do anything to help end racism. What did anyone here ever do to help me when I needed it? Nothing. No one did anything.

I'm terrified. I hear the small voice of my younger self in my head, the damaged one, and she really doesn't want me to be here. She doesn't like being seen as a target, so I always try to keep us safe, not set ourselves apart from others, especially when it comes to race.

But whereas my main mission is usually to listen to the child inside me, to keep us safe, today the louder voice I hear is George's. 'I can't breathe' are the words George repeated when he was being slowly murdered by white police officer Derek Chauvin. George's pleas for help fell on the deaf ears of this man and his three Minneapolis Police Department accomplices.

I can't breathe.

These words have given me the strength to silence the pleas of the scared little girl inside me. These words brought me here – to a place where I myself have felt fear. Where in my younger years I also found it hard to breathe, for fear of being targeted due to the colour of my skin.

I never feared being murdered – I am one of the lucky ones – but when I was out in town, my body, mind and soul were broken by local white people time and time again. It happened so often that I wanted to be invisible – no one can hurt me if they can't see me, can they?

I look up at the imposing Georgian building with its columns, its steps, its open forecourt where people perform and protest. It's impossible to hide here. How apt that, today, it is the site of the town's first Black Lives Matter protest.

In all my forty-two years, I have never attended a protest. I've never felt passionate enough about anything to want to protest about it. I've busied myself being a mum, business-woman and wife, diligently and dutifully fulfilling my roles in the constant pursuit of acceptance. I've done all these things quite well, I think, and have been congratulated for my superwoman-esque multi-tasking ability. I've even won awards for my achievements. But all the time I have been run-ning, both metaphorically and physically, from the trauma caused by my lived experience of rural racism.

My heart races as I walk around the corner to the front of this building. As I guessed, there aren't too many people here. The people of this town care more about saving the environment (it is the home of Extinction Rebellion) than they do about the lives of Black people. As I scan the pro-testors, I see one other Black person. He is not someone I know. Most of the people here, with their painted signs and face masks, are white. I keep my head down and seek out a friend, who promised me she'd be here.

As we stand together, face masks on and maintaining a two-metre distance (it's June 2020 and we are easing out of the first national lockdown), we talk about the events of the past week. My friend is a force to be reckoned with, and is super savvy when it comes to human rights and the importance of free speech. She helped me make the decision to come here when we both knew the protest would be seen by many as 'reckless', that we would be seen as putting people at risk of catching COVID-19. I needed an ally.

As we stand side by side, the protest organiser explains the schedule for the protest: 'It took eight minutes and forty-six seconds for George Floyd to lose his life at the hands of a white police officer and his colleagues. As a mark of respect, you are invited to take the knee while we hold him in our thoughts.'

Eight minutes and forty-six seconds is a long time. It's uncomfortable kneeling on a hard surface for that long. I try to keep the pressure on my knee light and change position, all the while keeping George at the forefront of my mind. I remember seeing footage of him pleading with Chauvin, begging for relief. I also remember the detached look on Chauvin's face. No emotion. No change in stance. No mercy.

My tears fall once again as I try to imagine how George must have felt, pinned to the ground by three police officers – two on his body (we didn't see them on the video) and Chauvin applying suffocating pressure to his neck. Even as George repeated, 'Sir, I can't breathe,' nothing changed. There was no reply to this Black man's calls for help.

I mentally replay the video of George calling for his

mama – she had died a few years earlier – and as I do the mother in me cries out silently as I think about my own twenty-two-year-old son. He too has been racially targeted due to the colour of his skin. This could be him, my boy.

Why did George call for his mama? Is it the safety and warmth of our mother's embrace that we want when we know the end is nigh?

With that thought, my 'be quiet and make everyone like me' defence mechanism – a strategy I have used to protect myself from re-experiencing the trauma of living with racism in this 'sleepy Cotswold town' for forty-two years – started to unravel.

As I stood up after those eight minutes and forty-six seconds, something inside me had changed forever. It was the straw that broke the camel's back.

The organiser asked if anyone wanted to speak.

I stepped forward.

'This town is racist . . .' I began.

1

FETE

It's 1988 and my village's fete is the community's 'come together' event of the year. It takes place every summer in the rectory gardens, an idyllic hidden space next to the church. You don't see the rectory gardens as you drive past or walk up or down the main road into town. You have to be a local to know it's there.

We don't play there much, to be honest. Even though the gardens are only about a ten-minute run from the flat where I live with my mum and sister, it's all uphill to get there – and anyway, there are plenty of fields around our place to explore, play tag and generally bum about.

The rectory gardens are the place for one thing and one thing only in my eyes: the annual community fete. The fete is the only event in the year – or the only event I go to, anyway – that brings people from across our village together. You get to see people you never see day to day. All sorts of people, too, not just people from down our road. It takes place every July, and the weather always seems to be good.

At the fete there are 101 things to do, from playing on the coconut shy to shooting BB guns at tin cans; from arts and crafts tables to the lucky dip; from cutest baby contests to biggest vegetable competitions. The organisers, who like to prowl around the fete in hi-vis tabards scribbling on their clipboards, do a great job at catering for everyone. There's always music in the form of a local band or school choir, and the smell of hot dogs, burgers and beer hangs in the air. It signals the start of summer.

But, at ten years old, all I really care about this year is who is going to be crowned the fete queen and her princesses.

The organisers of the fete, in their planning many moons ago, thought it would be a good idea to pick primary school children to be the fete queen and her two princess sidekicks. There's a whole procedure involved in this. The two village schools – ours and Trinity Primary over the hill – take turns to host the 'pick the fete queen and princesses' competition.

This year the competition is taking place at our school fete, and deciding whether to enter has been the subject of many a sleepover. I don't like entering competitions against girls in my school, especially when they're based on looks, because I am different. I am different to all the girls in my school. My hair is different, my skin is different, my nose is different. And my difference isn't a good thing. I am a blackie. That's one of the words they call me. I am fuzzy. I am not Daisy Hughes.

*

If I could be like one girl, if I could spend a day being one girl, it would be Daisy Hughes. Daisy is the most popular girl in our class. She's skinny with cute freckles, and she has the silkiest, most beautiful-smelling hair. Her mum puts it in neat plaits every day, tied with ribbons.

She lives with her mum, dad and her dead handsome brother in a massive house on one of the most expensive roads in our village. Everyone wants to be friends with Daisy. She has this aura about her. From the moment she enters the school playground in the morning, everyone wants to play with her. We all want to be around her. Want to soak her up.

Daisy goes on the most amazing holidays with her family. They go on planes. She comes back to school every autumn and tells us what they did, about places they visited and the new friends she made. Even on foreign holidays, people who don't even speak the same language as Daisy want to be her friend.

I struggle to get the boy who lives in the house opposite our flat to refer to me by my real name. He prefers to call me 'nignog'.

Anyway, I have it on good authority – from Daisy's best friend, Josie – that this year Daisy's mum has said that she can't enter the fete queen/princess competition. She's had the privilege of being picked quite a few times now – it's time to let another girl have a chance.

Rachel and I are hoping that the other girls might be us. Rachel is my best friend. She's my best friend because her mother and mine are best friends. Rachel is partially deaf and wears two hearing aids. I think she also has some kind of learning difficulty, as she gets special support in school, but I don't know. I don't need to know, because Rachel is my best friend and we've never fallen out. She's also one of the few girls I know who has never called me a name like 'blackie' or 'fuzz' or 'wog'. I feel safe when Rachel and I are together.

Maybe it's because she's deaf and has been picked on too – for things like not being able to hear people properly, or for shouting when she believes she's talking in a normal voice, or not understanding stuff as quickly as others. But when we're together, she's just Rachel and I'm Sabrina. She is a deafo and I am a blackie. We play and get lost in the worlds we create; we have best-friend sleepovers and parties.

It's late – nearly time for our midnight feast of crackers and jam. As we lie side by side under the covers in our nighties, we have the same conversation we've been having for the past few weeks.

'It's our last year of primary school, though, so we should at least try. Especially as Daisy perfect Hughes isn't going for it this year.'

It's true. The chance of us getting picked has increased somewhat with Daisy being out of the competition.

I sighed. 'I'm not pretty enough to be picked. I don't like it when everyone looks at me. You know I don't. It makes me itch when I feel that people are looking at me. They're not looking at me because I'm pretty; they're looking at me because I'm not pretty. They're looking at me because I don't look like the other girls. Like Daisy.'

'But what if this year they do want you? Because they're bored of picking the same girls like Daisy Hughes with the same old boring faces? And if you're not there, how can they even see you to make you the winner? You could be missing out on being queen because you're too shy.'

She was right. What if they wanted a different girl this year? All the girls in my school look the same – well, not exactly the same. They all have different colour hair, wear different clothes, have different teeth. But they're all white. So maybe the judges might want me this year. I'm a good girl. I'm polite, my teachers like me, and I'm good at school. Maybe it's my turn.

A little bubble of excitement started to build in my belly – but then I remembered our other commitment at the school fete: our popmobility dance display. Popmobility was the name of a free dance class that Rachel and I attended once a week after school. Each year, our dance group performed a routine at the school fete. Our dance teacher Fran – a woman in her thirties with a penchant for a green leotard and leggings combo – would accept no excuses for non-attendance.

'But what about the popmobility routine? Fran won't let us miss it. How will we take part in both?' I asked Rachel.

She smiled, knowing from my response that she might be winning me round. 'It would all work, I think. The dance display is normally way before the queen and princess competition. We'll have loads of time to get ready.'

'And we'll do it together. Me and you?'

'Yep. Beech Drive girls together. All for one and one for all.'

'Alright. If we'll be together. But I want to keep it secret until the day. I don't want any of the other girls to know that I'm going to enter, OK? Rachel, promise you won't tell?'

She held out her little finger. The streetlight shining through her bedroom window illuminated her white hand. I reached out with my little finger, and we intertwined them. Black and white.

'Pinkie promise,' we said simultaneously.

Most of the people who live on our road rely on social security benefits. Us kids – well, our single-parent mums – are in receipt of income support, housing benefit and free school meals. Any child who doesn't have much will tell you that that hot meal is the highlight of their day. It's mine. The puddings are my favourite.

Since we are a family on the breadline – or the poverty line – we don't often buy new clothes. Many of our clothes are hand-me-downs from friends and family or purchased from one of the many charity shops in town.

The intense excitement and joy I feel when opening a plastic bag of donated clothes stays with me to this day. It's like a mini-Christmas every time. My sister and I fight over who gets first dibs on rummaging through the contents, for we know that she who does will strut her stuff with aplomb, hoping that nobody will realise that the clothes are second-hand. Although we love receiving these clothes, we don't want people to know they're not new. If they do, then that makes us feel less than. As a low-income family, we don't need more of that.

To have some hope of being selected as a fete princess or – dare I dream it – queen, I know that I will need the best dress we can afford. I need to look neat, well put together. My dress needs to fit well and be clean and ironed. I don't want to give the judges any reason to knock points off for what I'm wearing. I want to look perfect.

I kneel in front of my drawers and look inside each one. Nothing here excites me. It's all too old, too dull, not pretty enough. I know the types of girl I will be up against. I've seen them at parties, how they scrub up, the effort their mums make so they are the belles of the ball.

I don't have parents like that.

Making myself perfect is something I must do alone. Nothing in my drawers is good enough. Nothing will allow me to shine. There's nothing I like, and nothing I feel the judges will like. I have to find a dress that will give me a chance. Help me stand out – for the *right* reasons.

The Nearly New Shop is the best charity shop in town. It's located just off the high street. Again, as with many places in this town, you have to be a local to know it's there. And – most important of all – to get the best stuff, you have to know the day they filter, tag and display the latest items. My sister and I shop here a lot, so we have the advantage. It's a Friday.

Charity shops have a certain smell. As soon as I walk into the shop, it hits me. That *l'eau de Charité*, a mix of dust, deodorant and – because our town has a hippy vibe – joss sticks.

The doorbell chimes, signalling my entry. The old woman behind the counter – because it's always old women who volunteer in charity shops – looks up, smiles a fake smile and quickly goes back to her book. I am a ten-year-old kid; she senses no threat here.

I manoeuvre through the narrow, overfilled aisles of the small shop, brushing past items placed so precariously that I fear even the slightest touch could unsettle them and send them crashing to the floor. There is a lot of stock here today. It's clearly been a good week for donated items. This shop is an Aladdin's cave of treasure for the taking – and right now I have first dibs.

But today I'm here for one thing only. As I walk towards the back of the shop to the kids' section and the rail of dresses, I hold my breath, close my eyes and make a wish. 'Please, please let the one be here. Please, God.'

When I open my eyes and focus on the rail, I see a mixture of pinks, blues, whites and yellows. I see polka dots, frills, ribbons. The rail is bursting with dresses of all shapes and sizes. I am so happy. My heart begins to race as I walk from one end of the rail to the other, a bubble of excitement building in my stomach. I reach out and skim my hand along the clothes, feeling cool, silk-like material, cotton, crêpe, buttons and zips. I close my eyes again in the hope that I'll feel drawn to a particular dress. I have played this game in this shop time and time again when picking clothes. I want the dress to find me. That's what happens in the films I've seen: the girl tries on a dress that transforms her from ugly duckling to the most popular girl in the school. When she wears the dress, people stop and stare – for all the right reasons. She's no longer a pariah, no longer something to be laughed at or someone to feel sorry for. She is the pretty one, the one they all want to be. I want that for me. Just for a moment. I want a dress that makes me feel like that. A dress that might make me a princess, or even a queen.

But back in real life, it's time to get to work. I start by pulling out all the dresses that are for my age. The fit needs to be perfect. I'm not as tall as Rachel, who always needs clothes for age eleven to twelve. I am not fat and not thin.

Now that I've picked out the dresses for my size, I need to get rid of dresses that I don't like the feel of or that feel too heavy. I know that being in the fete princess competition will make me itchy. When I feel under pressure, or when something bad happens to me, it feels like I have tiny ants crawling under my skin. I feel like I'm being eaten from the inside, and these ants are scuttling around my body. And then I start to scratch myself, because I can't bear the itch, I can't bear the ants. I scratch until my skin goes red. Sometimes it bleeds. So I can't pick a dress that feels weird on my skin because I don't want material that will irritate me further.

I get really hot too. Over the past year I've noticed that I have started to sweat, and that my armpits smell funny. Dresses and tops that are tight under my arms show the sweat, and boys in my class have laughed at the wet patches that appear under my arms. That cannot happen at the princess competition. The dress has to be a light material. That means the red velvet one won't work, so I put it back on the rail. The dress can't be tight under my arms either, like this light-blue sleeveless dress with the ruffled top, so that'll need to go back too.

I inspect the remaining dresses, back to front and top to bottom. This is important. The dress cannot have any blemishes on it. No stains, burns or marks. Most importantly, the dress has to be £5 or under, as that's all I have saved from the pocket money my grandad gives me each weekend. I have rationed buying sweets for the past four weekends, since the night Rachel and I decided to go for this together.

As I assess what's left, I say – almost in a mantra-like way – 'weightless, light, summery, pretty, weightless, light, summery, pretty'. Then I stop.

It's a pale yellow and dotted all over with small white spots, not too big and not too small – just perfect. I hang it on the rail and take a step back to look at it. The top half of the dress features a lace bib-like design. Four vertical lines of lace run from under the pristine white lace-edged collar down to the waistband. The skirt is flared. When I take the dress off the rack and move it from side to side, the skirt swooshes back and forth in perfect rhythm. And the dress has puff sleeves. I love puff sleeves – they allow me to sweat without it staining the dress, and I think a puff sleeve adds a regal element. Fairy-tale princesses almost always have puff sleeves on their ball gowns.

I turn it around to see a long silver zip. I test it by pulling the zip up and down a few times. It works smoothly and doesn't catch anywhere. The dress has passed all tests – all but the most crucial one. I need it to fit me.

I put all the other dresses back on the rail and head to the changing room. I close the curtains and hurriedly take off my jacket, T-shirt and shorts. I stand in front of the dress in my vest, pants, knee-length socks and beat-up trainers. *Please let it fit. Please let it fit.* I take it off the hanger, unzip the back and slowly step into it.

I turn my back to the mirror as I pull up the dress. I want it to be perfect. I thread my arms through the puff sleeves and bring the front of the dress up to my chest, holding the collar in place while I reach behind to zip it up. When I lower my arms to my sides, the dress falls into position. I move my hips from side to side, and the swish of the skirt against my legs makes me smile. I love the lightness of it, the way the skirt hangs perfectly. The sleeves don't constrict my arms. There's loads of space under my armpits. I puff up the sleeves to create the look I have seen on many a princess. I am ready.

Three, two, one . . .

When I turn around, the skirt swishes around my legs. When I take the first look in the mirror, I gasp. I can't stop looking at myself. The lace detailing. The contrast of the pale-yellow material against my dark-brown skin. How white the collar looks against my skin. The cinched-in waist. The regal puff sleeves. I feel pretty. I *am* pretty. I am a pretty girl.

I hold my hands up to my mouth and let out a quiet squeal. *Thank you, God, thank you, God, thank you, God.* I hold up each side of the skirt with my fingertips and curtsey as if I am meeting the Queen herself. In this dress, I would not feel ashamed to meet the Queen. That's how pretty I feel. And then I twirl round and round and round until I am almost dizzy. The skirt swings out. I imagine myself as a princess at a ball being twirled by her handsome prince, with people gazing adoringly at me because I'm so beautiful. That's me. That could be me. Maybe not with a prince at a ball. But as a princess, or even the queen, at the fete. I hope they think I'm beautiful too.

When I leave the Nearly New Shop five minutes later, swinging my dress in a plastic carrier bag, I have a spring in my step. I skip happily down the hill towards home, in a bubble of happiness and optimism. This dress could make me a princess.

The week before the fete, our school's normal timetable is thrown out of the window. Instead we are tasked with painting signs, making bunting, baking cakes, practising dances – country dancing is a very popular competitive school activity – and generally putting on the best show to convince our mums, dads and the community what rounded, well-behaved children we are. There is a party-like atmosphere at school. Our excitement builds at the thought of showing off our school – and, of course, finding out who will be crowned the fete queen and princesses.

The competition is all that the girls can talk about at lunch. Their mothers have purchased new dresses, ribbons and shoes for them. They know that they will be preened and polished to within an inch of their lives on the morning of the fete. Some even have their family hairdresser coming round in the morning to crimp and curl their hair. They're so excited. Surely someone around this table has a chance of being crowned at the fete.

There's nothing I can add when the girls are talking about how they will do their hair, so I remain mute. My afro hair doesn't behave the same way theirs does. I can't crimp it, curl it or wear it in a plait with pretty ribbons. I don't have a hairdresser or a salon that I visit with my mum.

I look down at my plate and push my free school meal around with my fork. I feel sad because I don't have a relationship like that with my mum. My mum doesn't know how important this fete is to me, because I haven't told her. I haven't told her because I don't want her to get upset about not having the know-how, or the money, to make me look prettier. I don't want to upset my mum because – no matter how much she wants to – she can't help me. She doesn't have the emotional or physical tools to.

My mum isn't like me. She's not Black. I get that from my dad. If he was here, I know he'd be able to help me with my hair, or at least take me to someone who could. He'd be able to show me how to look after my skin, to make it less dry. He'd cuddle me when I was upset and tell me about times when he was a kid like me and dealt with being called horrible names, or treated differently, because of the colour of his skin.

But he's not here.

My dad's not here because he left my mum – us – when I was a toddler and when my sister was a baby. He broke my mum's heart when he made that decision. The ripples created by his choice – days when my mum cries, chain-smokes, taps her foot on the floor repeatedly, goes numb and disappears into her own world – are hard on me and my sister. On those days we circle around our mum like birds, trying to protect her and keep her safe, afraid about what might happen to her, to us. How far down the rabbit hole will she go this time? Will she make it out? My sister and I hate it when she's upset. All we want is for her to be happy, so we try hard not to do anything wrong. We are good girls. We don't cause her trouble.

Not being able to help me to be my prettiest for this competition will cause my mum mental trouble. There's no way I'm sharing this with her, absolutely no chance.

Back in the lunch hall, I stay quiet. Of course I don't tell the girls any of this stuff about my mum. It's secret. None of their business. I accept that the conversation they're having is just one of many that I'm not qualified to participate in. I spear a cold potato with my fork and stuff it into my mouth whole.

When I get home, I go straight to my bedroom and look at my yellow princess dress, which is hanging up by my bed. I still love it, I really do, but listening to the girls talking about their new clothes and their pre-competition beauty regimes has robbed me of some of the optimism I felt when I first tried it on. Somehow my beautiful dress doesn't seem as beautiful as it seemed in the shop. I don't feel as pretty.

I've decided that I'm going to wear white ankle socks and my black high-shine loafers with the gold buckle. I would have preferred a new pair of pretty sandals, but I don't have any and I can't ask my mum to buy them for me. I place the socks and the shoes, which I have polished, at the foot of my bed along with a clean vest and pants. It's important that everything is ready for me to put on tomorrow after I have finished my popmobility dance at the fete. There's plenty of time between our group performance and the competition. Plenty of time for me to run home, wash, get changed and get back to the fete. I've worked it all out.

It's the day of our school fete, and I cannot believe what's happening. And it's happening because of a face-off between the owners of two overgrown courgettes, apparently. Why is this happening to me? Why is an overgrown courgette ruining my plans? Our dance set has been pushed back half an hour due to the 'best home-grown vegetables' and the 'bonniest baby' competitions running over. Fran, our dance teacher, is not at all bothered. 'Due to the princess competition and the mums and dads watching that, we'll have an even bigger audience,' she says. Fran thrives on an audience.

'Excuse me, Fran, but I want to enter the queen competition. I won't have enough time to go home and get changed if the dance time is changed. Can I sit out the last dance?' I plead with her.

'You're a key part of the group, Sabrina. You have to stay until we finish. You'll have more than enough time to get home and back before the competition. Don't worry.'

But I am worried. More than worried. With every minute that passes I feel that my dream is being pulled from me. And I don't have the voice or confidence to say no. So I just nod – 'yes, I should have enough time' – knowing that I definitely won't.

The final chords of the song fade away. My dance teammates and I stand in position, me on my knees with my hands poker-straight above my head, looking to the sky with a massive painted-on smile.

Fran instructs us to get up and lap up our applause, so we stand in a line and take one bow, two bows, three bows.

From the rapturous applause, it seems that our performance has gone down a storm. The audience are clapping, parents are whooping, and small children are trying to copy our moves on the tarmac, which is getting hotter by the minute in the intense mid-afternoon sun.

I whisper to Katie, who is bowing to my right, 'Katie, what time is it?'

She looks down at her watch. 'Quarter to three.'

I have just fifteen minutes until the start of the contest. It's not enough time, not enough time by half. I have to get home *now*. As Fran walks over to us, I decide I cannot stand here and listen to even one minute of her telling us how good we are, so I turn on my heel and run. I'll deal with her telling-off later, if that's what she wants to do. I need to get changed, I need to get rid of the smell coming from my armpits, I need to calm down and think pretty, regal, princess thoughts.

As I take a hop, skip and jump – just like Daley Thompson, that athlete from the telly – to the path which leads home, I stumble, twist my ankle awkwardly and let out a yelp. If anyone had told me then that many years from now I'd go on to run 250 kilometres, mostly alone, in the Sahara Desert, there's no way I would have believed them. My run slows from a sprint to an awkward jog as I try to take some weight off my sore ankle. *Bugger, bugger, bugger.* This is not good. I know, from watching these competitions for years and years, that the judges will ask me to walk in front of them as gracefully as I can. As I feel my ankle pulsating, I try to ignore the mounting pain and think positively. I don't have time for this.

Thankfully my vest, pants, socks, polished shoes and dress are there waiting, all pressed and clean, where I left them. I look at the digital clock on my chest of drawers: 2.51 p.m. I have nine minutes to change from a sweaty, smelly mess to something resembling a cool, calm girl worthy of a crown.

This was not how it was supposed to be. I was going to have a proper wash and condition my hair to try and make it look a bit softer, less Brillo pad-like. I'd planned to take time to calm down and say nice things to myself, not the hurtful things my mind can sometimes tell me. I wanted to recapture the feeling I had when I stood in the Nearly New Shop that day, when I truly believed I had a chance of being crowned a princess, or even a queen. But it's not meant to be. That sense of calm never comes naturally to me. I'm always on, always prepared, always fighting fire. Today is no different.

I pull at the buttons on my white polo shirt and rip it over my head. The red and blue ribbons Fran had attached with safety pins fall to the floor like leaves off a tree in autumn. I catch a whiff of my underarms and am blown away by the intense smell of my body odour, so I grab my can of Impulse and spray it so close to my underarms that the mist forms a white coating on my skin. I don't care; I need to hurry.

I step out of my blue dance skirt and kick it out of the way. Ouch, that was my bad ankle, and the kick has reminded me how much it hurts. I sink down on the matted pink carpet and very slowly take my white dap and ankle sock off my injured ankle. Using way too much time, I gently pull one long white sock onto my foot. I mustn't aggravate it any more. After doing the same for my other foot, I put on clean pants, vest and sparkling black patent loafers. Finally, I slip the dress over my head, pushing my arms through the sleeves and hastily doing up the zip at the back.

2.56 p.m. I have two minutes. I hobble into the bathroom and splash my face with water. I check myself in the mirror. I look hot. I look sweaty. I don't look pretty. But I don't have time to do anything more than run my fingers under the tap and wet my afro ever so slightly. This is my routine every morning. It normally takes about five minutes to get my afro to sit right. It's so dense that it keeps its shape. Kids at school tease me about it, calling me 'cone head' or 'flat head', depending on how I have slept. But it's not flat on one side now, it's uneven, so I quickly run my wet fingers through it and pull out bits that are flatter and pat down those that are too puffy. I know what I need to do but *I don't have time*. This is all I have time for – a thirty-second pull and pat. I want to cry.

I don't even want to look at the clock as I hobble to the front door. As I emerge onto the cold landing, all concrete steps and metal railings, and grip the banister to take the weight off my swollen ankle, I repeat, 'I am pretty, I am pretty, I am pretty.'

*

'Can all the girls *please* stand on the white line? Toes should be behind the line, and you should be able to reach out your arms to the side and not touch the girl next to you.'

I look down and put the toes of my shoes as close to the white line as I dare. The compère is frustrated that the fete is behind schedule. '*Please*, girls, do hurry up and stop faffing now, we have two princesses and a queen to find.'

When I lift my arms, I touch a hand and look around. There she is – my partner in crime, my best friend. Without her, I probably wouldn't have the courage to be standing here. Rachel. We share a nervous giggle and lower our arms, but as she looks ahead, I can't take my eyes off her. She looks so pretty. While I had to go to the charity shop for my dress, Rachel has a dress that knocks all the other girls' dresses out of the park. She's wearing a bridesmaid's dress. Yep, a peach bridesmaid's dress in the style of Little Bo Peep. It features three skirts – a hooped underskirt, a lace middle layer and a silk overskirt that glistens in the sunlight. The dress is puff-sleeved – much puffier than mine – and half off the shoulder, with little diamanté detailing on the front. She shines, and I want to be her. I've never wanted to be someone more than I want to be Rachel now. And she doesn't know it. She doesn't know how beautiful she is, how wholesome, how perfect. That's partly why she's my best friend. Because she's goofy, because she gets picked on too, she knows what it's like to be an outsider, but today she is worlds apart from me. So close to me, yet so far away.

'OK, girls, this is how things will proceed. Each of you will be asked two questions. The judges will stand where I am and will start with Girl 1, ending at Girl 15. The questions that you will be asked are: what is your favourite lesson at school, and why, and what do you want to be when you grow up? Once the judges have asked all girls these questions you will then be asked, in turn, to walk forward, turn and walk back to your spot. Is that clear?'

We nod. He's not to be messed with.

As the judges join the compère in the middle of the playground, I start to feel a tingling in my palms. A bead of sweat runs down my back. It seems to take forever for them to question the eight girls before me. I stand there getting hotter, sweatier and itchier.

When the itch starts, I always try to focus on something external. Today I choose the patch of tarmac just in front of me. I focus on that and mentally rehearse my answers. 'Creative writing with Miss Wright is my favourite lesson. Why? Because I love making up stories, creating new worlds and characters. I love using my imagination to dream up stories where good people always win. I get excited when I write, and Miss Wright says my stories are really good.'

I don't add the other reason I love writing, because I don't want them to think I'm weird or give them cause for concern. *But mostly I enjoy writing as it means I can escape from my life. I can pretend that I'm someone else – the lead character. I'm the heroine. And I love the feeling I get when I write.*

'Hello, Sabrina.' It's the compère, who, by day, is a teacher at our school. 'Since I know you, my fellow judges are going to ask you a few questions, is that OK?'

I smile and nod. Each judge asks me a question, listens then logs my response on their clipboard. My answers are faultless. When I open my mouth, I feel it's not really me; it's someone else speaking. Someone confident, someone intelligent, and someone who knows who she is. But it *is* me saying these things.

'A nurse. I want to be a nurse. I like caring for people. I love hospitals. The smell, the sounds and the buildings. I don't mind blood at all. I watch *Casualty* every Saturday night at my grandad's. I know that I would make a good nurse. If I continue to work hard at school, that's what I will be.'

The judges seem surprised. The compère, who knows me well, smiles, and I sense a feeling of pride in one of his students responding in this way.

'I have no doubt you will become a nurse if that's what you want, Sabrina Pace. No doubt at all.'

And with a wink from the compère, the judges move on to Rachel. I feel giddy. I know I did well. I did really well.

Once the questioning is out of the way, the compère and judges ask us to walk forward to the next white line, turn and walk back. Each girl duly obliges. They walk tall, their footsteps light and graceful.

Standing still has done my ankle no good. The first step I take sends a hot poker of pain up my leg to my hip. I wince and quickly shift my weight onto my other foot, but no matter how much I try, I can't walk gracefully like the other girls. I do my very best: I keep smiling, looking them in the eyes, looking forward, standing as tall as my swollen ankle will allow. I turn on the line, trying to get as much movement through my skirt as I can, trying to get them to ignore all that is wrong in this parade of mine. As I turn around, I see the smirk on Sadie Brown's face. Of all of the girls in my class, she's one of the worst for name-calling. The corner of her mouth is turned up and her shoulders are moving up and down. She's trying to stifle a laugh. Do I look that bad? Walking back, she is all I can see, even though I look ahead to my spot next to Rachel. I can feel Sadie's gaze burning into me.

After the walking section of the competition, we are asked to talk among ourselves and regroup in ten minutes to hear the judges' decision. The pain in my ankle is intensifying, so I find a spot on a bench underneath the tree by the school gate. A bit of shade is welcome, and so is the chance to rest. Rachel comes and sits next to me. 'I think me and you are going to be picked. I have a feeling.'

I look at her. 'I don't know. I think they liked my answers, but my walk was awful. My ankle hurts so much. Did I look really bad?'

'No. Not really. It was fine.'

I know she's lying. I know her too well.

'She looked like the Hunchback of Notre-Dame.'

I know that voice. It's Sadie. She's in the middle of a group of girls in the playground, and her voice is just loud enough for me and Rachel to hear.

'She'll never be picked. Why would they choose someone that looks like her over one of us? I'd never pick someone like her to be a princess. No princess I've ever seen walks like a disabled golliwog.'

They all burst into laughter. Like, proper belly laughter. I look down at my ankle, all big and fat, and scrunch up my eyes to stop tears leaking down my cheeks.

'Don't cry,' Rachel whispers in my ear. 'Don't let them see you upset. Especially her.' And she grabs my hand and squeezes it. We sit there, Rachel in her bridesmaid's dress and me in my yellow dress, waiting for the judges to call us back. Waiting for what feels like one of the biggest decisions of our lives.

As we stand on our spots, me next to Rachel again, the sun disappears behind a cloud. This brings relief from the glare of the sunshine, but also gives the decision a more sombre feeling – to me, at least.

'Thank you, girls, for being patient. This was a hard decision for the judges to make. You are all so wonderful this year. Your answers to the questions, your dresses, your hair – all of it perfect. I think this might be the hardest competition to judge for years.'

Please let it be me. Please let it be me. Please let it be me.

'Alas. We had to make a decision on our queen and

princesses. Mr Hedge, headteacher of Rodborough School, will announce the names of the girls who have been selected.'

I look at Mr Hedge, trying to catch his eye. Trying to see whether I can reach into his mind, control his voice and make him say my name.

'The competition was tough, girls. This has not been easy. But here goes: the princesses we have picked for this year are Rachel French . . .'

Oh my God, Rachel was right, we are going to be princesses, she was right!

'. . . and Anouska Williams.'

Anouska and Rachel. Rachel and Anouska. Not me.

I feel like I might faint. This was our thing. How can Rachel be picked without me? I turn to her and smile the best smile I can. 'Well done, Rach,' I say, before she and Anouska walk to the judges and are each handed a posy of flowers. I look at them standing there, this year's fete princesses. Beautiful girls with beautiful dresses and hair. The disappointment I feel at not being able to stand there with my friend, holding my own posy of flowers, is consuming me from my swollen ankle upwards. My legs feel weak.

'And, to complete the terrific trio, I announce our fete queen – Josie Price. Come on up and take your place between your two princesses. Come and receive your posy.'

The fact that the queen has been announced is of no consequence to me, because in my heart I knew that I would never be crowned queen. Princess was the best position I could have been awarded. And now, as they stand there for us all to see, the girls – my best friend and classmates, the girls who look nothing like me – I know that, no matter how pretty my dress, no matter how white my socks, no matter how much I tease my afro hair, I'll always be the odd one out. Always be the one to not get picked. Always be downgraded because of being me, because of looking like me. Because I don't look like the other girls.

And just like that, the competition is over. We disband. Rachel has to have her photo taken by the local newspaper photographer with Josie and Anouska, so I slowly start to walk – or hobble – back to our flat.

I spot the ice-cream stall at the end of the playground as I walk towards the gate. If anything can make me feel better, it's ice cream. My grandad always tells me to have a sweet when I hurt myself and, for a moment at least – and sometimes more depending on how much I eat – I do feel better. Sometimes I eat so many sweets that I fall asleep straight away once I have finished. It's so weird – after the initial sugar rush I get this funny feeling all over me, like pins and needles, like warm water. That's what I need now: some ice cream to see if it will make me feel better and less like bursting into tears.

I take my place in the queue and look at the price list. It's 25p for a cone and a flake. That's what I want to feel: the creaminess of the ice cream as it hits my mouth and slides into my throat, the crunch of the wafer, the silkiness of the chocolate flake as it melts. Saliva starts to pool in my mouth, and the pain in my ankle, and in my heart, eases a little.

They don't know I am standing three people behind them. At least, I don't think they do.

'The dark one – the one with the limp – she never stood a chance, did she? Poor kid. Growing up round here, looking like that? I wouldn't wish that on anyone.'

They don't say my name. They don't have to. I am the dark one. I am the only dark one here. And today, I am the only girl with a limp. The saliva in my mouth is replaced by a tightness in my throat. I've got to get away from here, back home, to my bedroom.

I silently retreat from the queue; I don't want the mums to turn around and see me, because they might feel embarrassed and I don't want them to say anything to me, to feel sorry for me, to say they didn't mean me. I always know that people mean me when they refer to 'the dark one', or when they say 'golliwog', or 'blackie', or 'fuzz', or 'flat head' or 'coon'. They always mean me. Because I am the only Black person here.

I hide behind the tree and wait for the mums to finish getting their ice creams. 'Go away,' I whisper, because I need to get out of here. I want to go home. I want to be safe in my bedroom. On my own. Once they disappear from view, I resume my walk of shame. All I can think is how, once again, I'm not good enough.

*

It is three more weeks until the community fete, when, riding aboard a trailer pulled by a tractor adorned with ribbons, streamers and banners, my best friend Rachel will sit beside Josie and Anouska and wave at the crowds lining the road, who will wave and smile back at them.

They will look down on the crowd from that trailer and they will feel special. Untouchable. Regal. I've spent the last week telling anyone who will listen that I don't care. That I'm happy for them. That they deserved it more than I did. That they will make wonderful princesses and queens. And every time I say it, my heart hurts. Because the words aren't true. I *do* care. I care so much. But my feelings don't matter, and they won't change anything, so I bury them away and only let my true feelings come out when I am on my own. All on my own.

'It's not gonna be the same without you,' says Rachel as we get ready for our dance class with Fran. 'Anouska thinks I'm stupid because I'm deaf and keep asking people to speak louder when they ask me how excited I am about being a princess alongside her. I can't help it if I can't hear them when they're too quiet, can I?'

'No, it's not your fault at all. I guess I've just got used to speaking a bit louder to you. It's natural to me.' And it is.

Fran bellows from the front of the school hall, 'C'mon, girls! This is not a mothers' meeting. I have exciting news following your performance at the school fete. Really fun and exciting news. Hurry up and get your PE kit on and get in line.'

What now? All I want to do is get this thirty-minute session over and done with, go home and pack for my weekly visit to my grandad's house. I need to see my grandad, to be with him and to be spoilt by him. And after last weekend – when I didn't see him so I could enter the princess competition – I have been yearning to see him. He makes me feel safe and special.

As we stand in line, she beams at us. 'Girls, after your brilliant performance at the school fair last weekend, I'm excited to tell you that we have been asked to *lead* the procession at this year's community fete!'

The screams of thirteen girls in a school hall are, apparently, quite frightening to our elderly male caretaker. Our shouts and squeals make Mr Price come running into the hall. He marches up to Fran, who is trying her best to make herself heard over our excitement.

'Girls, calm down. Calm down now.'

But for a good few minutes her pleas are useless and fall on deaf ears. So she uses another tactic. Loud music.

As the opening guitar riff to Eddie Cochran's 'C'mon, Everybody' belts out of the school hall sound system, one by one we shut up and calm down. We do this automatically, as we have been trained by Fran. Every time she plays a new piece of music that we are to learn a dance routine to, she says: 'Listen for the beat, girls. Listen for the rhythm of the music and feel it naturally move your body.'

As she paces backwards and forwards, she claps her hands

and moves her feet in time to the music. One, two, three, four ... one, two, three, four ... one, two, three, four ... one, two, three, four ...

'Can you feel it, girls? Can you feel the beat? It's so important to understand every prompt in this song. We can't afford to miss a beat when we're leading the procession.'

We all follow her lead, put our hands together and clap along, feeling the phrasing of the music in our heads, our hands and then our feet. As we stand in line following our leader, she changes her dialogue while still clapping and marching in time to the music. 'Step, bend, clap, step, bend, clap, out together, out together, one-two-three. Step, bend, clap, step, bend, clap, out together, out together, one-two-three.'

It's a rhythm that, by the end of the session, will be fixed in my memory.

'But one of us won't have a partner, Miss,' says Sadie, pointedly looking at me. 'There are thirteen of us, so someone will have to be left out.'

I look at the floor. My heart is starting to beat louder. I scratch my palms. *It's going to happen again. I'm not going to be picked. I'm going to be left out.*

'Well, that's where you're wrong, Sadie. One girl in our team can't be part of our dance troupe during the fete procession because she will be busy being a princess – isn't that right, Rachel?'

It takes a few seconds for Rachel, standing on my left, to catch on. 'Oh yes, Miss. I'll be on the trailer.'

I look at Rachel. She's not smiling as I expected. As we're dismissed from the session and walk to the back of the hall to get our bags, I ask her what's wrong.

'It's just that I'd rather dance with you than sit on a trailer with someone who thinks I'm stupid. I sort of wish I hadn't been picked now.'

I know I shouldn't be, but I'm secretly pleased that I now have this dance. And I'm pleased that Rachel doesn't. I know that makes me a bad friend, a bad person, but I'll live with that. Because now I have something to focus on and work really hard to perfect for the next three weeks. And I *will* be perfect. I'll show them all.

I work my bum off for the next three weeks. Every waking hour is spent thinking about the dance, listening to the song, finding the beat and practising the moves. How far apart should my step be, how wide should my star jump be, how quick on my feet should I be for my one, two, three? Every move has to be on point. It has to look seamless. It has to look perfect. I know every line to that Eddie Cochran song.

Fran has paired me up with Katie Bury. She's blonde and so white she's ghost-like, and she lives on the most expensive road in the village. I've been to Katie's for tea a few times over the years, but we're not that close. Well, not until we were paired up three weeks ago. Now, we're as thick as thieves.

'We need to do it like this, Katie,' I insist as I show her for the millionth time the move where we step forward, rotate our bodies and clap. 'We need to keep in line with each other. Because if you or I get too far ahead then it won't look perfect and we'll barge into the girls in front of us and that would be really bad.'

She rolls her eyes. 'I know all this. We've practised loads and I'm bored of practising. Shall we go to the shop? I have 20p.'

Although the allure of sweets is one I would normally cancel anything for, not this time. 'C'mon, Katie, let's just do it one more time. And then that's it before tomorrow. Deal?'

She gets up, slowly. 'Just once more.'

We congregate at the cattle grid just down the hill from the fort at 12.50 p.m. The procession is due to start at 1 p.m. Fran is frantically pinning red, white and blue ribbons to the sleeves of our white polo shirts while some of the mothers fasten red, blue and yellow ribbon bracelets to our wrists. I'm primed and ready, like a racehorse at the start of the Grand National. The nerves that are constantly present are surprisingly absent today. I feel calm. I feel good.

Although we know who our partners are, we don't know where in the group we will be placed. Katie and I talked about this last week. Who will we be placed behind – and therefore need to steer clear of? And who will be behind us?

And then Fran's voice, from somewhere in the melee, announces, 'Girls, the order of pairs today is as follows. From front to back, Sabrina and Katie, Sarah and Mel . . .'

I am at the front, I am at the front, I am at the front! I never thought I would be at the front. Second row, maybe, but the front? I don't get it. I'm not prepared for the front. No, I am. I am. I am prepared for the front. This is what I have practised like a demon for. *Believe in yourself, Sabrina* – that's what my teachers tell me all the time. So I have to believe that I'm good enough to be at the front. *I believe in you. I believe in you. I believe in you.* I close my eyes briefly and say the words, slowly and silently. Again, and again.

Fran stands at the front, facing us. 'Stand tall. Be proud. You have worked hard, girls, and this is your reward. Knock 'em dead!' A massive smile breaks across her face. I don't think I've ever seen a happier teacher. In return, we beam with joy.

And then the bass beat of 'C'mon, Everybody' starts to boom from the mobile speaker mounted on the safety car in front of us. It's show-time.

Every step I take is on point. Every star jump is just right. Katie and I are totally in sync and we smile as we catch glimpses of each other. We know that we're doing well. All that practice, all those hours are paying off. I get a little excited when we round the corner by the Prince Albert pub and I see my mum and sister clapping along. They look proud. They came!

All the spectators are smiling and clapping. What a sight we must be. Me, the dark one with the fuzzy – but very well-rounded – afro and Katie, the blonde-haired, pale angel-like being. Although we are different, we are the same right now. Our feet move the same, our hands and bodies move the same. We are being applauded because we're good. Because we're a sight of perfect synchronicity. Shadows of each other.

I wish with all my heart that I could bottle this moment, because I am *so* happy. For a moment I don't feel the sadness that always feels like it's a breath away. I don't feel different here. It's strange: I feel like I belong here. Maybe not being picked as a princess was fate. Because right now, I know I'm exactly where I'm meant to be, and where I want to be.

I never want this feeling to end.

2

THE BUS RIDE

Adam Norton, Christian Philpott and Graham West.

Three boys who, for two hours a day, from Monday to Friday, make my life a complete and utter living hell.

My new secondary school, Richmond Hill, is 5 miles away from where I live. Because we get state benefits and my mum doesn't drive, I still get free school meals and, now, a free school bus pass too. How lucky am I!

I hate the fact that I have to go to this secondary school. Of all the schools the local education authority could have sent me to, this is the worst one for me. The absolute worst. Because not one other person from my primary has been sent here with me. No one. So I'm totally alone. Every single kid in my class has gone to a secondary with at least one friend. All except me. How is that fair?

But that's not even the worst thing about being sent there.

A boy I hate goes there too. Grant King. He's three years

older than me and lives on my road. For as long as I can remember, Grant has enjoyed making me squirm by calling me names and intimidating me when I'm out playing with friends. If Grant is around, I can't relax. I can't have fun. I have to be on guard. If I see him playing outside, I stay inside. It's that bad. I don't like it when he stands in front of me and spits 'nignog' and 'coon' right into my face. He laughs at me when I tear up, and I feel stupid for being weak.

So getting the letter this summer to say I've been accepted to Richmond Hill was like receiving my death warrant. When Grant sees me at school, I'll be his plaything. Something to amuse himself – and his friends – with.

In my mind, I *should* be attending the local all-girls grammar school. Mr Hedge, my primary school headmaster, told me I was a definite. 'Sabrina, you're exactly the kind of girl who will do well at this school. You're a shoo-in.' That's what he told me, and my mum and I believed him. More fool me. It turned out that I wasn't intelligent enough to pass the entry test. And, since my mum hadn't picked any other schools she'd like me to go to, I got Richmond Hill.

Since I received that letter, I've stopped believing anything that teachers say – in fact, all adults. They lie to make me feel better about being crap. They all do it, but they shouldn't because it sets me up for more heartbreak. Why do adults do that?

It's the fourth week of the new school term. As I slam the door to our flat, my safe haven, I start to get anxious.

My anxiety is manifesting, as it always does, in 'the sweats'. It starts at my head and then, just like always, appears at my armpits.

My afro hair keeps the heat captive, near to my scalp, and it turns into tiny beads of sweat. I can feel them forming. I can feel my forehead getting damper. My National Health glasses are starting to slide down my fat negro nose.

I bet that a 'normal' girl's hair behaves itself. I've studied my friends' hair and girls I sit behind on the bus. White girls have thinner hair, hair that seems to be better at letting heat escape. Their heads cool faster, and sweat doesn't pool as fast as it does on my scalp. It's not fair.

My little sister, Sharon, has normal hair and looks white. Even though we have the same mum and dad, my sister and I look totally different. The only thing we have in common is the NHS glasses we both wear, due to our short-sightedness.

So many times, growing up with Sharon, I have wished so badly that I was born as her. My sister's hair looks nice in a ponytail. She can have a fringe. She gets freckles. Her skin goes red in the sun instead of getting blacker. To my knowledge, she has never been called a nigger, because that's not what people see when they look at her.

Sometimes I look at her and I don't see how we can be sisters. I love her loads, but I have this recurring dream – which I've had so frequently that I often think it must be real – where I see my sister with my mum and her real dad, a white man. Her looks finally make sense to me.

'Ah,' I say to myself. 'That's why we don't look the same. Because we have different dads.'

I just can't understand how she and I have the same mum and dad, yet she looks white and I look Black. How can that be possible? I don't get it. All my friends share physical characteristics with their brothers and sisters – teeth, eyes, hair colour – but not me and Sharon. As I said, we only share bad eyesight.

I hate it when people call me names in front of Sharon. She panics and doesn't know what to do because she's younger, smaller and can't stick up for me. I don't expect her to. That's not her job. It's my job to protect *her*. I also sometimes wish, and I know this is bad of me to say, that she looked more like me. That she had my hair, my nose, my skin. That I could be a big sister who comforts her, and gets comforted in return, when people call us the same horrible names. That we could share ideas on how to deal with people like Grant. That we could share the load. Because that's what I see Black people do on TV: they share stuff with their family and friends. They have people to turn to who say, 'I get it. I've experienced that too.' I don't have that with my sister, and I don't know any other Black people to talk to either. I wish I did. Every day, I wish I could talk to someone – anyone – who looked like me.

As I walk to the bus stop, my afro acts like an insulation blanket wrapped around a hot water bottle. I'm overheating and I've only been walking five minutes. Shit, I can feel more and more sweat droplets forming on my hairline. I bet they'll release when I really don't want them to. This routine of overheating and sweating isn't new; it happens to me every day on my walk to the bus stop. Monday to Friday, just like clockwork. I know it's my body's physical reaction to having to get ready for the bus ride to hell.

I've got to try and reduce the intense heat that's building up inside me. And now – oh, here we go, it's phase two. The itch. The overheating is always followed by the itch. As I walk to the bus stop, sometimes the itch hits me so hard that I scratch at exposed areas of my skin – on my wrists, mainly – so intensely, I bleed. I've scratched a bit of my outer layer off, the half-caste outer layer, and with it comes one of the things that cause people to be mean to me.

As I dab my finger on the scraped skin and the drop-lets of blood, I feel a weird sense of release. I can't explain the feeling but it brings, if only for seconds, a moment of calm. I know it's weird, but I feel better for it. I also like it when the blood scabs over and eventually falls off: when it does, it leaves a silver scar on my skin, and for a time that area of me looks whiter. I look a little bit like everyone else I know. It's only a small part of me, but it's something at least.

I'm dithering, playing for time, and I'm going to be late for the bus, so I quicken. This change in pace is no good for my overheating, though, and now my armpits are starting to pool with sweat. I know the damp patches on my school shirt won't smell so much this morning, but when I get on the bus at the end of the day I'll smell – and I really don't want the bullies to have something else to attack me for.

I get to the bus stop with five minutes to spare. Five minutes to compose myself. I need to remember to be still. Be oh so still and oh so quiet. Today, I won't play ball. I'll look ahead and be brave. It's only an hour. It'll all be over in just an hour.

'Alright, wog.' Grant is standing behind the tree having a crafty cigarette. He's looking directly at me. As he does, he smiles and exhales smoke rings. It's been four weeks and he knows as well as I do what's ahead. He calls me a name and leaves it at that. Something to wake me up.

I can see the big green double-decker bus approaching out of the corner of my eye, but I continue to look ahead. What if I step out in front of it? Will I be killed? Or will I just get badly injured, which means I'll have a few months off school? That'd be nice. If I just stepped forward right now . . .

Honk!

The sound of the bus's horn snaps me back to reality. The bus stops just in front of me. The driver's face is so red and angry that I think he might spontaneously combust.

'CAN YOU SEE THROUGH THOSE GLASSES? You're going to get yourself killed standing that close to the kerb!' he shouts at me. 'Did your parents not teach you anything?

If I ever pull up here and you're standing that close to the kerb again, I'll tell the school.'

Maybe if he did, I'd be expelled. That'd be good.

'I'm sorry. I didn't realise how close I was,' I lie.

Out of the two bus rides I have to take every day, the return journey is the worst. I dread it. During my morning journey, my tormentors are normally still sleepy, meaning they haven't had time to plan their attack. Come 3 p.m. and the final bell, it's game on.

'Oi, wog. Nigger. Oi, nignog. You – you, down there. Don't you know your name?'

I keep looking ahead, staying really, really still. I'm not going to cry today. *Sabrina, don't cry today.*

'Answer me when I speak to you, girl. Your master is addressing you, Nigga.'

Every day it's the same. In the first few weeks of school I hoped with all my heart that they'd get bored of me, tire of my monosyllabic answers, if I even answered at all, but they haven't. Their thesaurus of racist taunts grows and they use so many new words, words I don't even understand, to make me feel like utter shit. I hate myself more and more each day for not having the strength, or vocabulary, to answer back.

Their bullying gives them such pleasure. They laugh and congratulate themselves for each critique of me. Sometimes people I consider friends join in and laugh with them. When this happens, I feel even more alone. I have no allies. There is always such joy on their faces. This time of the day seems to be their favourite.

A bead of sweat trickles from the nape of my neck down past my collar and onto my back.

One.

The lads – or the three amigos, as I non-affectionately call them – revel in finding new ways to humiliate me, single me out and chip away at me. Do they know, or care, how much they're hurting me? And if they do, why do they continue? Does it make it worse that they might know the effect they have, yet they continue their daily attack on me anyway?

'Coon, are you mute? Did your master take your tongue? Did you talk back and the master took your tongue? C'mon, Fuzz, talk to us. Tell us about your day.'

Two.

Another bead of sweat springs forth. I focus on what I can control, and I think cool thoughts to stop the overheating. I imagine that my heart is a block of ice and, with every beat, the coldness of it is seeping through my veins, slowly cooling all my internal organs and finally my skin. I *must* stop the sweating. I *must* slow my breathing.

The three amigos have endured a day of school, a day of being told what to do, so they want to let off steam. I am their pressure vent: their taunting of me is a way to release the tension that has built in them during the school day. I am a dartboard, and every arrow they throw is aiming for the bullseye. Me breaking – or crying – indicates that they've hit their target and won the game.

'Are we making her cry? Is she going to tell on us? Tell her mummy? Poor little black girl.'

Three.

I have to stay as quiet and still as I can. I am as still as those people you see in Covent Garden who look like statues, painted grey all over, and then, when people walk past them, they move and scare the shit out of them. I need to be that still and that frozen.

Four.

Why is it the same every fucking day? The amigos never tire, never focus their energy on anyone else. Why can't they pick on someone else to give me a break? I mean, I'd be bored of just focusing on one person by now.

But they never tire, and it's always me.

No one sticks up for me much any more. My friends have tried in the past, but they end up being called names like 'nigger lover' and it makes everything so much worse. The amigos are even crueller when they feel they have an audience, so my friends and I decide that ignoring them is the best course of action. My best friend Jo often sits beside me, looking forward too. She silently supports me, squeezing my arm when she can see, or smell (due to my underarm sweat pooling), my anxiety getting the better of me.

I try every tactic in the book not to encourage them. I

ignore them but they just get angrier, shout louder and call me 'deafo'.

I pretend I'm confident and engage in conversation with my friends in the hope that the amigos won't bother with me. It doesn't work; they just throw things at me.

I sit downstairs on the bus, but they find me and manoeuvre their way next to me. They whisper, 'Fucking black hoe' in my ear and tell me how disgusting I am, how no boy will ever want to be my boyfriend. Their words are like angry wasps burrowing in my ears and repeatedly stinging me.

Five, six, seven, eight, nine, ten, eleven.

Not sweat any more. Tears.

To cry is to show weakness, and I try so hard not to. When the tears come, the amigos know that they've got me. I try my hardest to stop my tears from falling, but I can't seem to manage it today. At home, I practise stopping myself from weeping. I've been studying the art of showing no emotion for weeks now. I call it my 'being numb' time. To practise this I listen to really sad songs and watch sad movies. I imagine my mum and sister dying in tragic accidents and me being left alone. No matter how much it hurts inside, I practise stopping myself showing it on the outside. I don't move my face at all; I swallow my tears and I let my mind drift off somewhere else. *I cannot let the emotion show.*

I'm getting better at being numb when someone hurts me, I really am. But today it hasn't worked.

When the amigos know they've won and got what they

want – which is me staring straight ahead, tears flowing, dead inside – they stop. Their mission for today is complete. To be resumed tomorrow.

The 'coon' has been broken.

I need to get home to my safe space, and practise even harder for tomorrow.

3

SASSENACH

'You're nae buckin' daughter o' mine. Never set foot on
Scottish soil again.'

A father wrote these heart-breaking words to his
seventeen-year-old daughter. Less than three months earlier,
she had fled her home town, leaving everything she knew,
everyone she loved, for a new life, a better life, a life of
freedom.

His hurried, angry handwriting was scratched ferociously
into the cheap, lined notepaper. He'd written the letter after
he saw the photograph of his daughter, Mary, in the arms
of a Black man.

That was Granda's reaction when he saw a photo of my
mum with my dad.

The year was 1977. Three months prior to this exchange my
mum, Mary, had left her home town of Hainsburgh – a tiny
blink-and-you'll-miss-it Scottish ex-coal mining village. She

craved so much more from life than Hainsburgh could offer and, after a tumultuous adolescence involving petty crime, running away and other misadventures, she decided she had to leave.

She left as soon as she could afford to, and as soon as she could persuade her fiancé, Stevie, to go with her. She had got engaged at sixteen – not unusual for girls in her village – to a boy who adored her and would do anything for her. It didn't take much to convince him to go along with her plan. He didn't want to leave; he loved his life with her in the village, but he'd do it for her. Anything for her.

So, at seventeen years old, they did just that. With only their pay packets for the month in hand, they packed their bags and got on a bus bound for England – Manchester, to be precise.

When Mum and Stevie arrived in Manchester, Mum was dizzy with excitement. It was such a big place – the lights, the people, the buzz of the city. She fell in love immediately, even though they had to spend the first night in an all-night diner as they had nowhere to sleep. Stevie, on the other hand, was not so enamoured. She knew he wasn't comfortable here but ignored it, because for once in her life she felt free. Manchester was all she'd been craving.

The couple found places to stay the next day in the form of hostels – one for men and one for women. The situation wasn't perfect, but it ensured a bed, a bath and warmth. Weeks passed by happily – for Mum, anyway, who was revelling in her new life, quite happy playing at being an adult and living off benefits.

But Stevie became more homesick as each week passed. He missed the routine of village life, his family and friends. So of course the inevitable happened. Mum wouldn't, *couldn't*, give up her new life for him. She handed the engagement ring back and he – her only link to her old life – headed back home.

My mum was alone, apart from a few close friends she had made while staying at the women's hostel. One, Carol, had moved in with her boyfriend Tony, and Mum often found herself hanging out at their place. It was here that she was introduced to Simon, a young Black man who worked with Tony.

She didn't realise until Carol told her that Simon, this dark, handsome stranger, had taken a shine to her. Mum had never met any Black people before. Hainsburgh was a very white community. In fact, the only people of colour she had spoken to before she met my dad were the Pakistani shop owners in her village. But that was all about to change, as nineteen-year-old Simon had fixed his sights on getting to know her, no matter how many times she shied away from being alone with him.

The first few times he asked her out, she made excuses. She'd never been with anyone that looked like him before – a Black man. She didn't know why he liked her. Her anxiety about the unknown – and her unconscious and conscious bias – made her back out of the first date she agreed to go on. She hid behind the sofa when he came calling. My mum, the girl who wanted freedom and moved to Manchester to find it, hid behind a sofa to dodge a Black man who simply wanted to get to know her.

Thankfully, the next time she agreed to a date she took a leap of faith and turned up, buoyed by her friend Carol. After spending the evening with Simon, she wanted more. More time with him. More conversation with him. To be with him 24/7.

Within weeks, they were falling in love. Time spent away from each other was time wasted. They soon moved in together to a love nest in Stretford Road. They were so happy, and Mum wanted the world to know.

Then she decided to write a letter to her sister, telling her all about her new life in Manchester – and her new relationship. She included a photo of them together. In love. It was this letter that provoked her dad's reaction.

She sat on their bed, reading and rereading her dad's angry letter, holding it in shaking hands, rocking back and forth, crying. Nothing Simon, who sat next to her, could say or do could take the pain away. To be banished from her homeland for falling in love, to be ostracised from her family because of the colour of Simon's skin – this was a reaction she hadn't expected. Knowing her proud Scottish father as she did, this was it. There was no going back. Mum knew that no one would be able to change his mind, not even his wife. She'd seen him turn against other people, including family members, and she could see him in her mind's eye relaying his disgust – 'No daughter o' mine' – to anyone who would listen.

She was a pariah. And all because she fell in love with a Black man.

In the months that followed, my gran kept in touch with Mum by letter, expressing sorrow for the way her husband had reacted but no more than that. She didn't promise to talk him round. She avoided mentioning what had happened. She just asked politely about Mum's well-being.

During this time, my mum and dad decided to move from Manchester to Taunton, my dad's home town. He'd only moved to Manchester – to a probation house – as he'd got in trouble with the law for fighting, but he'd served his time and wanted to go back home. What they knew, that no one else did, was that my mum was pregnant with her first child – me.

For Mum, moving to Taunton with the man she loved – the father of her child – was a no-brainer. For who else wanted her now? Who else would welcome her, her boyfriend and their unborn child? Mum was Roman Catholic and she loved my dad dearly, so there was never any question of not keeping me, even though she was only seventeen.

My dad lit up like a Christmas tree when she told him she was pregnant. He was so happy. He had been fostered at a young age, and prior to that he'd been in a Barnardo's children's home, and he wanted to be the father he never had – until he was fostered by his white foster parents. He couldn't wait to show his child the love he felt was lacking in his early years. To be a proper family. Doing that in the town he called home, when Mum had been banished from hers, was the first step in the right direction.

When they arrived in Taunton, my parents moved in with my dad's foster parents, Brian and Eileen Brewster. Very quickly my mum developed a close relationship with them and, since she had no familial support at the time, they became her surrogate parents. They of course asked what her relationship with her own parents was like, and she told them. What did she have to lose?

When he heard how Mum's father had reacted to her relationship with Simon, Brian – one of the finest men you could ever meet – took it upon himself, after seeking my mum's blessing, to compose a letter. This letter – five hand-written pages – was the first act of white ally-ship I ever encountered. And I hadn't even been born yet. His love for my dad, my mum and me – his soon-to-be first grandchild – transcended any fears he had about writing to the proud and angry Scottish man he had heard about.

An intelligent man who worked in senior management at British Telecom for most of his working life, Brian sat down that day with a pen and paper and did his very best to com-municate why his boy, Simon, was a good lad: a lovable young man with a heart of gold who wanted to be the best person he could, despite having endured his fair share of trauma and tragedy from a young age. He said he understood the conscious and unconscious racial bias my Scottish grandad had towards Black people. He wrote about how in the 1960s he and his wife Eileen, a white married couple, had fostered three children – two Black, one white – and due to this had experienced more than their fair share of racial abuse.

My nanny, Eileen, had told me about numerous occasions when people verbally abused her while she was pushing my father in his pram. They shouted cruel misogynistic and racist comments about her and her child. They would spit on the ground and cross the road to avoid them. Why? Because they believed she had cheated on her white husband with a Black man. What else could explain what they saw – a white woman caring for a Black child?

To them, it was wrong.

In his letter my grandad said he understood why Simon and Mary's relationship had come as a shock, but he encouraged Granda, by sharing his own lived experience, to put his racial bias to the side because Simon deserved a chance. When my mum saw the letter, before it was sent, she cried – tears of gratitude and of love for the man she had only known a few months. This man who was fighting for her, Simon and the baby.

Brian never received a response. No acknowledgement from across the border.

'What else can I do to help?' he would say to my mum.

'Nothing. Once my daddy makes a decision, there's no going back.'

She truly believed that.

New Year 1977

Every year, as was tradition in Scotland, my mum's family would come together and party hard to see in the bells. That magical time when the clocks strike midnight on 31 December, ringing out the old and in the new. A time for friendship, family and reflection.

For the first time, Mum was missing the traditional Hogmanay celebrations. Instead she was in Taunton, seven months pregnant, hundreds of miles away from all she knew. She felt melancholy. She tried to shake the feeling, cheering herself up by reflecting on how the last twelve months had changed her. And although she felt proud that she had achieved all she set out to do when she left Scotland, and she felt freer than she ever had, she felt an emptiness too. Because she couldn't share it with them.

The phone rang in the room next door. Eileen got up to answer it.

'Mary?' she called. 'Mary, it's for you.'

Mary was confused. Who would be calling her now, so close to midnight? It must be Carol, her mate from

Manchester. 'Hold there. I'm coming,' was her reply as she hoisted herself out of the chair and waddled to the other room.

'Hello?'

'Hiya hen, it's yer mammy. I wanted to call and wish ye a happy Hogmanay. We're all here at yer Auntie Mary's and we're thinking of ye. Are ye alright?'

Shocked at hearing her mum's voice, Mary was silenced for a second, unable to respond due to the lump in her throat. Finally, her voice came back. 'Aye, Mam, I'm fine. I'm just here wi' Simon's mammy and daddy, waiting for the bells,' she responded.

'Listen, hen, I've got somebody here who wants to speak to ye.' The line crackled, and then she heard it. His voice. The one she'd never expected to hear again. Neil, her dad.

'Aye, alright, hen.' His voice. She hadn't heard his voice in months. It felt like a lifetime.

Her hands shaking, she gripped the phone close to her ear. 'Aye, alright, Daddy.' Her voice was weak and childlike.

She could tell from his initial words that he was well oiled, deep into his traditional Hogmanay bender. For many Scotsmen she knew, it was a bender that would last for days.

'Whit are ye bucking up tae? Yer mammy telt me aboot the wain. Aye well, ye look after yerself, hen, and get ye and that bucking grandwain up here next year. Are ye hearin' me?'

She *was* hearing his words, but she couldn't believe them. Her father was going back on what he'd said. Inviting her back to Scotland. Giving her permission to go home with her baby, his grandchild. Was this really happening? Was the call even real? She pinched herself to check.

Her voice was wobbly, quiet from shock or relief, emotions she didn't yet understand. 'Aye, Daddy. Aye, I'll be up after the wain comes,' was all she could mutter.

'Aye. Well, happy Hogmanay, hen.' His voice broke – was he crying? The line crackled again.

'Alright, hen?' It was her mammy back on the phone.

'Aye, Mammy. I miss ye.' Pent-up tears were breaking through.

'Aye, hen, I know. Listen, I dinnae want to gie yer auntie Mary a big phone bill. I'll gie ye a wee ring soon, OK? Love ye, doll. Happy Hogmanay.'

And with that they were gone. The glimpse into her old life, the connection to her family – terminated. As she stood there, phone in hand, she knew instinctively that Brian's beautiful, thought-provoking letter had played a part in this surprise call – this olive branch from father to daughter.

'Alright, my love?' Brian said as she re-entered the sitting room.

'Aye. It was ma daddy.'

His bright blue eyes sparkled, watery for a second, and he smiled. 'All OK?'

'Aye, it's alright,' she said with a sigh. He winked, took a sip of whisky from his glass and smiled. Simultaneously, they returned their stare to the television as the announcer started the countdown. *Ten, nine, eight . . .*

*

I was born on 28 February 1978 at Musgrove Park Hospital in Taunton. My little sister Sharon came along two and a bit years later.

The first thing my mum did after having me was call home. Her parents didn't have a phone, so she left a message with Mrs McCafferty, the next-door neighbour, to tell Neil and Nettie that Mary had a wee lassie.

Five months later, she felt ready to introduce me to her family. In England, she knew her life. Loved her life. She had her routine, her friends, and had made a home. Up in Scotland it was different, unpredictable. But she had to go. She and her mum had been exchanging letters and calls and Nettie was desperate to meet me. So she decided to return – just her and me, no Simon on this occasion. Mum wanted to protect him, to see the lie of the land.

The train ride was nine hours long. As she arrived at each station – Birmingham New Street, Wolverhampton, Crewe, Carlisle – her nerves got worse, her nausea increased. She hadn't heard a thing from her dad since Hogmanay. Had the conversation ever happened? He had been drunk. Did he even remember it? Was she really welcome? She'd asked her mum all these questions.

'Aye, hen,' was the response every time. 'He wants tae see ye and the wain.'

But did he? How would he react? *No daughter o' mine* had been the words he'd used. And the baby – how would he be with the baby? Her world. Her beautiful girl.

'Motherwell is our next station stop,' said the conductor over the tannoy.

This was it. She'd fed and changed me for this first meet and I had been sleeping soundly for the last hour of the journey, with not a care in the world. Mary, however, was becoming more anxious as each second passed. As the train slowed into the station, her heart was beating faster, thudding loud in her ears. Her mouth dry. *Just stay on the train, Mary. Get off at the next stop and go back home to Simon.*

And then she saw her mammy. It had been almost twelve months since she had seen her face, and she had missed her desperately. Nettie, standing there looking into each train window as it passed, suddenly spotted her daughter and started to run to her.

Stepping off the train, babe in arms, my mum ran into her warm embrace. Nettie welcomed her daughter and her mixed-race baby back onto home soil.

'Hiya, hen.' She kissed her on the cheek. 'Oh, let me see her. Oh me, oh my,' she cooed as she took me tenderly out of Mum's arms. 'Look at this wee gorgeous. Hiya, hen, I'm your wee granny.' A smile spread over her face and tears gathered in her eyes as she cuddled me close, pulling away the white woollen shawl I was wrapped in to see me properly. Mum carried our bags, with help from my gran's next-door neighbour and close friend, whose husband had driven them to the station.

Just then, Mum realised that he was here too – her daddy. He had come to pick her up as well. She could tell that he had been drinking. She'd got used to seeing the signs all her life. Living with familial alcoholism was part of her DNA, a generational norm.

He barely looked at her, or at me, as she entered the car. She slid across the back seat, wanting to shrink into the corner of the car, away from him, from any hurt he could inflict, wanting to protect the baby.

'Aye. Was it an alright journey?' he muttered as the car got going, his words slurred, his voice high-pitched.

'Aye, Daddy, it was fine.'

He craned his neck round, his gaze darting towards her face then down, trying to get a look at this Black baby, his grandchild.

'Aye, well, ye'll both be tired, hungry tae. I think we've got a bunch o' bananas in the fridge.' He smirked.

'Hoy, sir, that's fucking enough. You'll no' speak to the lassie like that in ma motor,' the driver said, loudly, forcefully.

My mum just sat there, every word he said piercing her vulnerable heart. It seemed that her worst fears were real-ised. Was this how it was going to be? Far from the relative safety of her new home, far from Simon. As she cuddled me close, she wanted to shout, 'Turn the fucking car around, I'm going home!' She wouldn't – couldn't – let him do this to her, or her baby. Her eyes bored into the back of his head as she thought of all the things she'd always wanted to say to him, all the times she stayed silent – even before Simon – times when she should have spoken up, told him, told all of them.

'That's *enough*, Neil.' Nettie's voice boomed out, strong. It was an order. And with it he knew, the whole car knew. Her command to him was about what he had just said – and so much more. For the way he had treated their daughter, for the time they – she – had missed supporting her firstborn's pregnancy, and for all the times she, as his wife of twenty years, should have spoken up and didn't.

They all sat there in the car in silence. Finally, when they passed the signpost for Mum's home village my granda responded quietly, 'Aye, Nettie. Aye, ye're a hell o' a woman.'

Granda never again referred to the colour of my skin as something that set me apart. My granny had told him that was enough, and he heard her.

During the two weeks we stayed in Scotland, his love for me and his protectiveness grew. Neil Cairney, one of the best men in the village, had a Black grandchild, and she was to be accepted.

'Oh, she's a bonnie wain,' the family that gathered to meet me said. 'A wee doll, our Mary. Well done, hen.'

One day, when she had taken me to the local shop, Mum forgot to put the brake on the pram and off I went, hurtling

down the pavement. The pram flipped over, hu
swaddled in blankets, into the road. Locals who
it rushed to my aid.

'Check the bairn! Is she hurt? Where's her mammy?'

In the short time it took for Mum to check me over
and, in shock, push me back to her parents' house just up
the road, they were all there waiting: about ten members of
the family, including Granda, who was the angriest of them
all. He grabbed me while lambasting her for her stupidity,
raging that 'anything might hae happened tae the wain'. His
grandchild. Beenie Bunch, as he came to call me.

During that visit Mum felt like things got back to normal –
or as close as possible, considering all that had transpired.
Later that year, after she and Dad were married – none of her
Scottish family attended – she took her new husband home,
and Neil met Simon.

When someone who looks nothing like anyone you've
ever seen in real life comes to your tiny village, that someone
becomes the talk of the town. Especially when to most of the
women – and a fair few of the men – the dark, handsome
stranger is the spitting image, even down to the long leather
coat, of the 70s movie character John Shaft.

Simon Pace, Mary's husband and the father of Neil's
grandchild, got tongues wagging and net curtains twitching.
Of course, everyone knew about Neil Cairney's initial reaction
when he heard of his daughter's relationship. But now the locals
were falling over themselves to take Simon for a drink in the

...o ask questions, to congratulate ...'t matter to them that he could ...y said, their Glaswegian dialect ...ty of back slaps, handshakes and ...n' for him to get the message: if ...was good enough for them.

My dad's first trip to Scotland was a resounding success. He was a charmer, and he left Scotland feeling he'd impressed his in-laws and done right by my mum in spending time with her family, her father in particular.

My mum was elated – delighted by how he had conducted himself and how he dealt with meeting the people she loved – the people who had banished her from Scotland – and proud of them as a couple for showing them all. Her decision to follow her heart and leave the village had been the right one. Her life right now showed that. She had found freedom, love, and was living her dream. Things were rosy. As they boarded the train back to Taunton, she thought that things could only get better.

But my mum's happiness didn't last long. Heartbreak, it seemed, was always waiting for her. Upon their return to England after the trip to Scotland, the council allocated my mum and dad their own house. Finally, a home of their own. So far they had been living with my dad's foster parents, all on top of each other, and they craved their own privacy. Finally, it seemed their prayers had been answered.

Their first year in their new home was happy, or so Mum thought. She busied herself being a dutiful wife, making sure the house was clean, I was cared for and – most of all – my dad was looked after. He worked to provide for us, and she worked to create a home, a safe space for us all. It seemed that all the pain she had endured had been worth it. She was in love with the man of her dreams and, to top it all off, she became pregnant with their second child.

A few months later, she felt a gut instinct that something wasn't quite right. It was nothing she'd been told or had found – well, not at first, anyway – but every morning when she woke, she felt sick. It wasn't like the morning sickness she had experienced in the early days of this second pregnancy. It wasn't hormonal. It was fear.

Nothing that she could put her finger on had changed at home, but Simon wasn't himself. He was often distracted. Even when he was with her, he wasn't mentally there. And, if she was being honest, this change had happened since he'd stopped wearing his prescription NHS glasses, when his confidence had soared. As soon as he'd ditched them for contact lenses, there was a marked difference in how people, especially women, looked at him. Women were brazen. They would do a double take when they walked past him, giggling, sometimes wolf-whistling, even when my mum was by his side. He'd laugh, lapping up the attention, and in those early days my mum would too. Because he was hers.

Until she found out that he wasn't.

It started with rumours. No one came out and told my mum that he was having an affair, but the insinuation was there. One woman's name kept being spoken in relation to her 'being a troublemaker'. Mum asked Dad about the rumours and about this woman, and he denied everything. Deny, deny, deny. He told her there was nothing to worry about. She wanted to believe him. With her second baby due soon, she was scared about being alone, so she left it.

My sister arrived in the spring of 1980. For the following year, things seemed more settled. Simon stayed home more, being the doting father that Mum wanted him to be. But as time wore on, he became restless. That gut feeling she had experienced before returned. My mum's fears were confirmed a few months later when, on hoovering the family sofa, she found an unfamiliar necklace. Her world came crashing down. After months of anxiety, countless denials from Simon, and questioning her own sanity, she finally knew. He had brought a woman to their home. How could he do this to her, their girls, and here, in her home? Her heart was broken. It was the ultimate betrayal – of her, of their girls, and of the sacrifices she had made in choosing him.

She didn't tell him she'd found the necklace; she was too hurt by his infidelity to mention it at first. Foolishly, for a few weeks he asked her whether she had found anything while cleaning.

'No,' she replied. And each time he asked the question, her hurt would turn to anger, her love to hate. But she still didn't say anything. She liked seeing him sweat, the cheating bastard. One day she decided to take the necklace and pawn it, keeping the money for herself, for her and her girls, because they deserved a treat.

My mum lost all trust in my dad. Over the following months – after many arguments in which she accused him of having affairs – he finally admitted some of them. Although she never told him that she'd found the necklace and pawned it, she did tell him she knew he'd had women in the house. She said their marriage was over and he had to leave. It was just after my sister's first birthday.

Six months later, heartbroken and unable to carry on living in the same town as him and hearing about his exploits, she decided to move with us, aged three and one, back to Scotland. She stayed there with her parents for a month, until, due to being classified as homeless, she was given a first-floor council flat. She believed it would provide her with the healing environment she needed.

It didn't. A single mother with two small children, she struggled to cope with being back here in this small village. She felt she'd failed herself and her children. Broken, her dreams shattered, she sank into a depression.

We stayed there for nine long, dark months. Mum hated herself, her life, and the situation she found herself in.

Brian, who was heartbroken that he didn't see us every day, would call Mum regularly to check how we were. A religious man who wholeheartedly believed in the sanctity of marriage, he was full of sorrow for his son's conduct. Of course, he was still in contact with my dad who, by then, had found himself a bedsit in Taunton and was living the life of a single man, intermittently calling Mum to check on the welfare of his children. Each time he did and she heard his voice, her heart – struggling to mend – would shatter all over again.

Brian had recently retired from BT. To be nearer to members of his family, he and Eileen had moved from Taunton to a small Cotswold market town. He saw an opportunity to help my mum make a new life and to see us, his beloved grandchildren, more regularly.

'Come and live with us, my love,' he said to her one day on the phone. 'We have space in the house. Come and stay until we find you somewhere else.'

Mum's mammy could see just how wrong her daughter's decision to come home had been, and helped Mum make the final decision. Mum had outgrown the village. It was plain for all to see. And her return – to the place she had fled – was crushing her daughter's spirit and, in turn, impacting on our well-being.

'That's enough now, hen. Get yourself, and the wains, together and away fae here. Hainsburgh isnae doing ye any favours.'

It wasn't an easy transition. Brian would lovingly remind her when he could see she was subdued to 'give it time, my love'. This new town wasn't like Taunton, with its bustling promenade, parks and vibrant nightlife. This place was rural.

'In the sticks', some might say. It took a few months but Mum finally found a rhythm to her new life, made new friends and eventually – even though Brian begged her to stay with him and Eileen – a new home for her and her girls. The darkness that had felt all-consuming started to release its grip on her.

Since we were poor and unable to afford trips abroad, we spent every summer holiday visiting our family in Scotland. As soon as school ended, our suitcase would be packed, train tickets booked, sandwiches made and off we'd go.

I am one of fourteen grandchildren on my mum's side. One of the best things about going to Scotland was seeing my cousins. As soon as we reached Carstairs train station, just across the border, my sister and I would be giddy with excitement. We'd pinkie-promise each other that we wouldn't argue for the whole holiday. We'd talk excitedly about eating our favourite Scottish foods, cuisine that you couldn't get in England – things like fruit pudding, square sausage, my granny's soup, tablet, Scottish ice cream and Irn-Bru in glass bottles. We loved it all.

But each year I became more aware of how different I looked to everyone else, and so my excitement was mixed with a lot of anxiety.

It was different for my little sister. I envied her white skin and the way people treated her. I was so jealous of how easy she found it to meet new people, like our cousins' friends. Sharon wasn't fearful about meeting other kids, like I was; the only things that scared her were the bogeyman and the dark. She would go straight out to play with my cousins, leaving me to watch them out of the window as they skipped off. I spent more summer holidays than I care to remember sitting alone in my granny's house, in her armchair by the front window, watching my sister, cousins and their friends go to the park or to hang around at the bus stop. When they eventually came home, I'd hear about what they had got up to.

People really did treat us differently. With Sharon, the Scottish kids found her English accent strange, as it was so different from theirs. They'd ask her to say phrases they found funny, like 'hello, my love'. But if I went out to play, they'd ask me to raise my arm so they could compare their skin to mine. They'd comment on how light they were and how dark I was. Or they'd touch my afro hair and laugh at how springy it was, and invite other kids to do the same. That didn't happen to my sister. And sometimes, when I was tired, grumpy or sad, I would be mean to her because of it. I would pick fights with her. I'd pinch her when no one was looking, just because I wanted to make her feel the way I did.

In the weeks before our holiday, I'd hound my mum.

'Mum, don't make me go out and play if I don't want to, OK?' I'd make her promise. 'I just want to play with my cousins. I don't want to go and play with strangers.' I reminded her constantly, to the point she'd get annoyed with me. But I needed her on my side.

She'd tell people I was shy. When my cousins asked me to go out and play with them and their friends, and I said I didn't want to, my mum would say, 'She's just shy, hen.'

I wasn't shy. I was scared of being targeted, and I didn't want to have to deal with being upset by strangers on holiday: kids who were mean to me with their words and their stares because I was different, Black and not like them.

This was my holiday. This was when I was supposed to be able to relax and get away from the racism I experienced every day back home. To be with people who loved me for all that I was – fuzzy hair, dark skin, glasses and all. I didn't have the strength left to deal with racism here too. For me, it was a time to recharge. So, no, I didn't want to play out.

The kids in Scotland didn't call me the same names as the ones back home. At home I was nigger, coon, wog. Up here I was wee darkie, blackie, ya wee black bastard. My cousins, if they heard any name-calling, would always jump to my defence but, as far as I was concerned, that wasn't their job. They shouldn't have to do that for me. It wasn't fair on them. Why risk their friendships just to defend me, their darkie cousin? I'd just make up excuses to go back to my granny's, where I'd lock myself in the toilet, cuddle myself and cry silently so no one would hear me.

I was relieved when they gave up trying to get me to go. For me, happiness was sitting at my gran's feet, in her scullery, listening to the fast chatter of my aunties and uncles. It made me feel safe and relaxed: when I was there, no one could hurt me. My family loved me for who I was – most of the time, at least.

But confrontation was always waiting, even in safe spaces. And when it came to my Scottish family, it was always triggered by alcohol. Granda could be one of the sweetest, most loving men when sober, but give him a bottle of Eldorado and a few cans of lager, and he could rip you to shreds in seconds.

'Hoy, Beenie. Wee Beenie Bunch. Get in here the noo.' His voice was high-pitched above the records playing in the background – a sign that Granda was entertaining his friends once again. 'Hoy, ye. Ye Sassenach! Get in here.'

On one occasion, he'd been drinking since early afternoon, having gone out dressed smartly and clean shaven. My gran, used to this routine, had been cleaning all day. It's what she did when she was anxious or worried; she couldn't sit down.

'It's ma nerves,' she'd say. She would silently pray that he'd just want something to eat and then go to bed when he eventually came home, but on this occasion, like so many others, he wanted to party. Three of them had returned drunk, Granda and two of his best friends, each one holding a 'carryout' – a plastic bag full of lagers and spirits.

My gran, mum, auntie and us kids were tucked away in the small scullery, keeping out of the way with whispered words and nervous laughter. We were fearful of Granda's unpredictability after he'd been drinking. Like the flip of a coin, we knew that joyous laughter could turn to fist fights and blood. We had to be ready.

'Beenie. Buckin' get in here the noo.'

Gran looked at me. 'Go on, hen. See what he wants and then he'll leave ye alone.'

I got up and walked slowly into the living room, the lion's den, where the smell of spirits, smoke and cheap aftershave hit me square on.

'Hello, Granda,' I said timidly as I stood in front of the fire, opposite my gran's statue of Jesus on the cross. Christ and the three drunk men were looking at me.

'I want tae ask ye a bucking question. Whit are ye?' Granda used to say 'bucking' instead of 'fucking'.

'I'm Sabrina, Beenie Bunch, Granda.'

He looked at me, his red cheeks darkening. 'Dinnae be smart wi' me, lassie. Whit are ye?' he repeated, anger in his voice.

I didn't know what the right answer was, what I had to say to go back into the scullery, to safety. My heart was beating faster and I felt hot and itchy. He was getting annoyed with me, and I didn't know what to say to pacify him.

'I'm Beenie Bunch, Granda,' I stuttered, looking at him, wide-eyed, pleading for that to be the correct answer. Beenie Bunch was his nickname for me – I'd never thought to ask why.

'Aye, you're Beenie Bunch.' Angrier now, his tone accusatory. 'Are ye English or Scottish, ye bucking Sassenach? Whit are ye?' He was shouting, spitting words at me.

'Hoy, Neil, that's enough o' that. Let the wain go back tae

her mammy,' said the man to his right, winking at me as he tried to calm Granda.

My knees started to tremble. I clasped my hands in front of me, scratching my palms hard as I looked at him. I knew what he wanted from me. I knew what would placate him and quell his boiling rage. He wanted allegiance. Assurance of our perceived identity. Our nationalism.

I knew I was English. I was born in England. My father was English. England was my home. But I was Scottish too. That was my genetic heritage too. I was 50/50. Mixed. I was half-caste. I wasn't a complete person. I didn't feel I belonged anywhere. But all I wanted was to belong. To be accepted.

'I'm Scottish, Granda. Just like you,' I said too loudly. I felt that maybe raising my voice to say it, to convey a sense of pride, would please him, and then he'd let me go. It felt like I was on trial. I was in the dock and these men were my judge and jury. 'I'm not English, Granda. I'm Scottish. I am.'

He was staring into my soul. Looking for the lie, for any chink in my armour to show him that I might not be telling the truth. His piercing dark eyes searched me. I was paralysed on the spot.

'Aye. Scottish ye are.' His voice less harsh now. 'Ye're some lassie.'

I breathed again, not even realising I'd been holding my breath. I think I got away with it.

'Aye. This lassie is Scottish.' He turned to the jury and

spoke. 'She can recite a wee Scottish rhyme as well, can't ye, Beenie?'

'Yes, Granda,' I said. 'Do you want me to do it now?' Now, I was less defendant and more court jester, his fool. He looked back at me. 'Aye, hen.' He leaned back in his chair, chest puffed out, a tot of whisky in his hand.

Don't mess it up, I think.

Summoning up my best Scottish accent, I recited, 'It's a braw, bricht, moonlicht nicht the nicht, Mrs Richt. Are ye no thinkin' of buying a toaster?'

With that all three men, led by Granda, laughed out loud. The tension was immediately crushed. His friends even raised their whisky glasses to me.

'Aye, hen. Ye're Scottish alright. Ye ken?' said the third man. I smiled. Looking again at Granda, I silently pleaded, *Can I go now? Please let me go now.*

'Aye. Well done, Beenie Bunch. Ye're some lassie.' He chuckled. 'Gie yer granda a peck.' He pointed to his alcohol-blushed cheek then turned it to me. I leaned down to his chair, his throne, and kissed him. Neil Cairney, the King of Scotland – and me, his minstrel, my duty fulfilled for one more day.

As I walked away, I heard him say, ever so quietly, 'Aye, ye bucking Sassenach.'

I was wounded again. Mocked. Nothing I did was ever good enough.

I knew what 'Sassenach' meant because I asked my

gran when he first called us it. It means 'English' and it's a
term – and not an endearing one – that Scottish people use
to describe the English.

When someone you love others you, it hurts so much.
Instead of using my skin to set me apart, Granda used my –
our – Englishness. He knew we didn't like it, yet he still did it.
He seemed to derive some sort of pleasure from it – but only
when he was drunk. This routine of us having to justify our
nationality went on for years. As I got older and developed
my own liking for alcohol, my trips to Scotland became less
traumatic and full of anxiety.

As my cousin happily told me, a few swigs from a bottle
of Buckfast – a medicinal wine supped by Scottish youth
looking for a cheap hit – would give me the confidence I
needed to hang out with her and her pals. Being out more
meant that Granda couldn't call upon me to prove my allegiance, and I wouldn't have to perform for his love. Win-win.

Drinking was standard in Scotland. Habitual. Everyone
did it, because there was nothing else to do in small Scottish
villages like Hainsburgh. Drinking gave me the courage I
needed to feel normal. Just like them. To not be the shy
person they believed I was. I learned to be the person *they*
wanted me to be, even if that meant losing myself. They still
called me names and compared their skin tone to mine and
touched my afro hair, but I let them because it made them
more comfortable with me. My feelings didn't matter; I just
wanted their approval. I became a chameleon: I was English,

Scottish, Black, half-caste, the carer, the good daughter. For years I voluntarily split my soul into pieces in order to be accepted, even by those I loved.

It worked for a while, until the coping mechanisms I had spent years refining began to destroy me.

4

DON'T TOUCH MY HAIR

'She's cut my hair to make me look like the Fresh Prince of Bel Air!'

I can't believe I've allowed this to happen. I have allowed this woman – this white woman – to butcher my hair. This silent assassin has used her machete, assuming the outward form of a pair of scissors and an electric razor, and butchered my afro.

It's 1991. *The Fresh Prince of Bel Air* may be one of the most watched sitcoms in the world but I, at thirteen, absolutely *do not* want to look like his lighter-skinned twin sister!

I'm speechless. I just don't know what to do. I feel paralysed in my own body. It's such a weird feeling, like there's an invisible force pressing down on me, squeezing the air out of me. I'm really struggling to breathe. My heart is beating fast in my ears. I am in fight-or-flight mode, and it's terrifying.

Oh my God, the three amigos are going to eat me for breakfast! I really am dead meat now. It's so fucking hard at school anyway – and now this. I feel bile rising from the pit of my stomach: a massive bubble of acid, slowly rising, passing along my intestines, coming for me.

'You OK, love? Can someone get you a drink?'

A drink? Is she serious? Can she not see with her own eyes what she's done to me? She has no bloody idea that she has signed my death warrant right here in this salon. She's signed it with a pair of sharp scissors, acting as a pen, poised in her nimble fingers. She has committed an act so barbaric that there is no coming back for me.

I politely request a glass of water.

I must control myself. I must slow down my breathing. I must not be sick here in the chair. Breathe in – one, two, three – and out – one, two, three. But this feeling won't go away and I'm getting scared. Scared that I am going to vomit right here on the black and white tiled floor of my hometown's Snazziest Salon.

She could see it in my eyes, the desperate fear of a customer on the brink. The wide-eyed, pinpricked death stare that says: 'WHAT THE FUCK HAVE YOU DONE TO ME?'

'How close do you want me to shave the sides, love? We can go grade 1 or grade 2?'

Please, I beg you, don't shave the sides of my hair. I plead with her silently because, of course, I can't say these words out loud. My mum has raised us to be nice girls. To be polite, to always say please and thank you, and to be respectful to adults. And, most importantly, not to cause trouble. My dialogue is internalised: I cannot upset the white woman and 'cause a fuss'.

I know that causing a fuss leads to heartbreak, pain and suffering, so it's important for me to remember to remain small and mute.

'I think it is fine as it is, thank you very much. I don't want the sides shaved too close. I really don't want the colour of my scalp to show,' I say meekly.

PLEASE HELP ME, SOMEONE. PLEASE HELP ME. OH MY GOD, OH MY GOD.

I'm not sure how this situation came to be. My mum normally cuts my hair. Well, I use the term 'cut', but really she just shapes my afro with kitchen scissors and a paddle brush into some warped homage to Michael Jackson in his early Jackson 5 years.

My mum has never understood how to manage my Afro-Caribbean hair. I don't think I remember her ever speaking to anyone about it. No one Black, anyway. Her lack of skill is evident in all my primary school photos. I make sure she hides them away in a drawer because the memories of 'look at the blackie's Brillo pad hair' still sting. I don't want a constant visual reminder of how different I am to her and my sister when I'm at home. All I want to do is try and forget.

So yes, I'm getting fussier about my looks. I have to take charge, since no one else will. I'm sick and tired of being a target, and my hair is always the first thing that people comment on. They want to touch it, they want to hide things in it, they want to see if they can get their plastic combs through it. I need to do something. I can't change the colour of my skin, no matter how much I keep out of the sun or wash myself until my skin bleeds. But I *can* change my hair.

'Mum, please, please can you make an appointment for me? Please, Mum? With someone who knows what they're doing? I promise, I'll get a paper round or something to help pay for it.'

I thought that if I enlisted the services of a professional hairdresser, my life would instantly get better. I wouldn't be targeted as much, and I might get a bit of rest from the name-calling if the bullies see that my hair can be styled just like theirs. If I show them that I'm really trying to blend in, to be like them, maybe they'll like me more.

So here I am, sitting in this leather chair, all hot and sweaty and feeling like I'm in an invisible choke-hold.

'How flat do you want me to make the top, love?'

Oh my God, she's going in with the clippers. She's lawn-mowing the top of my hair!

'Please don't take too much off.'

Why can't I speak up? Why am I being polite to this woman? She's ruining my life. I am never going to live this down.

Five minutes later, it's over. What feels like the abuse and desecration of my soul.

The stylist smiles and chats to me about how 'cool' I

look, while angling her large mirror to show me the back, the front, the sides, the top.

I die inside.

'This town's female version of the Fresh Prince. Your mates will be so jealous.'

FUCK. MY. LIFE.

I run home like I'm Linford Christie, almost tripping over my legs, they are going so fast. I'm the human representation of the roadrunner bird as I hurtle under the railway bridge, past the builder's merchants, around the corner by the vet, and sprint along the track to the steep field that leads to our flat. *Beep beep!*

I keep my head down as I run; I don't want to make eye contact with anyone. I don't want to see their pitying stares or hear their suppressed giggles. I'm not emotionally ready. Keep your arms pumping, Sabrina! Don't stop until you get to your safe space.

No one is home when I get in, and I'm glad. I need time alone to process the horror that I've allowed to happen to me. I need to be able to cry if tears come, here in my safe space, as I have done on my own so many times before.

I sit on my bed and can hear my heart pounding so incredibly loudly in my ears. I am on the verge of vomiting from the combined mental trauma of my new haircut and the physical effort of my run home. I tentatively pick up my make-up mirror, keeping the reflective side face-down on my lap for a moment. I need some time, a moment to create a new space in my Pandora's box – a place deep inside me where I store all the things that hurt me, to be dealt with at a later date – for the potential terror that I know awaits me on the other side of this mirror.

Maybe I dreamed it. Maybe I never even left this room. It can't be as bad as I think it is. I do this when bad things happen to me – I pretend that what's happened isn't real. That it's happened to someone else. But what if this time it really did? Yep, I think I dreamed it. I never even left our flat.

I lift the mirror and look back at my reflection, and see what has happened to me, what I have allowed to happen to me. This is no nightmare; this is real. My own inability to stand up for myself has caused this and – yes – it is worse than I thought.

Tears sting my eyes. My vision blurs. As I stare at my foggy reflection, a featureless being stares back at me. Big, fat sorrow-filled tears run down my cheeks as sobs I don't quite recognise as my own rise from my chest.

They're going to crucify me.

It has taken four months for my hair to grow out, and those four months felt like a lifetime. I'm not going to lie and pretend things aren't a hundred times worse for me, because they are. There's a renewed vigour in the racist slurs that are targeted at me. I've brought this on myself and have absolutely no one else to blame.

People called me 'Fresh Prince wannabe' for a little

while, but now they've reverted to 'fuzz'. Kids who are casual acquaintances and even friends call me 'fuzz' too. I've lost all the confidence I had, and that wasn't a lot to begin with. I self-identify as 'fuzz'. I internalise their words and claim them as my identity. There's no point fighting it. I am no longer Sabrina. I am fuzz, I am wog, I am nigger nose. I try to make them think that their words bounce off me, like a tennis ball hitting a bat. I perfect the art of laughing it off. I store away the pain to process later on, somewhere safe, somewhere alone.

One Saturday every month, to escape the small market town where I live, a few friends and I get on the train and head to the nearest city, Gloucester. It feels like another world. In Gloucester there are Black people, brown people, Asian people and Indian people. They just live their lives. I don't get called out here; they don't get called out here.

In Gloucester I am free!

My confidence soars because I'm not the odd one out. Plus, Gloucester has a Tammy Girl, a department store and a McDonald's! What more could we want?

Today I have persuaded my friends to walk with me to Barton Street. This area of the city has a bad reputation – created, in the main, by white folk who feel uneasy walking down a street where there's a high proportion of people of colour and shops, cafés and convenience stores that cater for them. Barton Street is seen as an unsafe 'do not travel alone' territory when, in fact, it's nothing of the sort.

I am a girl on a mission. I am looking out for InStyle Hair Salon, a salon specialising in Afro-Caribbean hair. I called them from a phone box earlier in the week and booked a consultation with a stylist. I've been saving up my pocket money for four months and, last week, I finally saved enough for an initial consultation and 'steam treatment'. I have no idea what a steam treatment is, but the woman on the phone told me it was a 'deep conditioning treatment' and it would be a good 'place to start'. So I booked it.

Tentatively I open the salon door. I'm instantly hit by the sounds of Gloucester FM (a Black-owned community radio station playing R&B, hip-hop, rap, jazz and reggae), the happy chatter of staff and customers – Black women, men and children, and the smells of hair cream, perm lotion and chemical straightening treatments. The attack on all my senses is overwhelming and I feel quite heady.

I'm scared and I don't know why. It doesn't help that my white friends are huddled together, their gazes darting here and there, as if they're going to be pounced on any minute. Maybe now they might understand how it feels to be me among loads of white people. They're forever telling me to 'ignore them and face your fear' – ditto, friends, ditto!

I give the receptionist my name.

'Your stylist is running late. You can either return in an hour, or wait here in the salon.'

I can sense that my friends want to go, but something

inside me feels rooted to the spot. I can't leave. I want to take this all in.

'Why don't you walk back into town? If I don't meet you by five, just get the train home. I'll be fine to get the next one,' I tell them.

My friends stare at me with a sense of disbelief. They know me to be incredibly shy in crowds. They know I hate feeling exposed, but something feels different here. I feel I need to do this alone, and I can only cope with my own anxiety at the moment, not theirs too.

'You sure, Sab? We're happy to stay.'

I know they're actually not; we've been mates a while and I can tell. 'No, honestly. You go. Finish shopping. I'll be fine.'

And with a smile they're gone.

'Sabrina, do you want to come and have a seat over here?'

Fiona is a Black woman of about thirty-five. She has an athletic body, strong jawline and the most beautiful braids, which flow from her scalp right down to her waist. Tight, thick braids that I know will have taken hours and hours to weave. I know this as I have researched how to create braids, having tried to do them on myself. It didn't work out well.

I sit down and feel that familiar bubble of anxiety building in my stomach, my heart beating faster, beads of sweat starting to gather.

'Have you had a treatment before?'

I feel shy and extremely unsure of myself in her presence. 'No.'

Fiona runs her long fingers through my hair. With every stroke, I feel more and more ashamed. I can tell from the way her fingers are getting stuck that she can feel the matted lumps that have formed in my hair from four months of me pulling it back into some form of ponytail. Most days I don't even bother to brush it. I hate my hair. She gently runs her fingers around my hairline, inspecting the breakages at my scalp from too much pulling. Sometimes, when I wake up in the morning after another night of my hair being pulled back, I take the hairband out and wish with all my heart that my hair would just stay straight. It never does; it just bounces back up. A fuzzy mess.

I'm ashamed of myself, of the state that I've let my hair get into. I lower my head and feel my eyes start to water.

I must try not to cry. I must try not to cry.

I feel hands on my shoulders. Strong hands. Giving my shoulders a gentle squeeze, Fiona says, 'Sabrina, look in the mirror. What do you see?'

My head feels too heavy to lift. An incredible sadness has swallowed me up and I feel paralysed once again.

I force myself to look up. 'My hair is matted. I see a half-caste person with matted hair.'

I'll never forget the look Fiona gives me. It's a look of sheer anger, mixed with sadness and compassion. As she bends down behind me, lowering her gaze to mine, she says in a voice that I know all the salon can hear: 'You, my beautiful girl, are *not* half of *any* caste. I *see* you. I SEE YOU!'

I only realise at this moment that I've been waiting my whole life to hear these words.

My world turns on its axis.

This woman. This stranger has me pegged within five minutes of meeting me. She saw through my defences and has peered into my soul. I swear she knows the battering I have taken over the years. She knows that I feel worthless and utterly lacking in self-esteem but – most of all – she knows just how much I need a Black person, a Black woman, to *see* me, to empower me. With those words, she gives me a taste of that, and I know that this is what I have needed, have been craving.

It is a pivotal moment in my life.

I spend four hours in her chair that day. It takes that long for her to gently tease the knots out of my matted hair. I see a bead of sweat roll down from her brow, thanks to the force she's having to apply to get the wide-toothed comb through my hair.

Bit by bit my hair loosens, drops, and then I see the real length of my afro. For the first time in forever, I feel my hair touch my shoulders. This must be what a proper girl's hair feels like, I think. I liked it, a lot.

I'll never forget leaving the salon that day. I felt lighter, freer. As I walked down the street, two teenage boys who were walking together parted for me and – as I passed – one of them wolf-whistled. The joy I felt was intoxicating. Things were going to change, I just knew it.

I went to see Fiona in her salon for years. I loved my appointments with her. She never knew it, but I loved her like a big sister. I loved her fierce nature, her sass, and the way she made me feel. I felt powerful in her presence. And I loved being with people like me. I referred to her as Aunty Fi because she told me that, in Black culture, people often refer to older women who have proven to be wise as 'aunty'. The work she did with my hair was miraculous, but the work she did on my self-esteem was out of this world. Each appointment with Aunty Fi was educational, empowering and transformational. In that chair she shared with me Black history, stories of slavery, stories about notable Black civil rights activists such as Malcolm X, as well as information on our region, where to go and places to see. She also taught me how to look after my hair, my skin and – most importantly – my soul.

I finally felt a sense of community, of togetherness, and it was addictive. Fiona taught me the importance of owning my identity, of being confident enough to identify as a Black person. Of finding my own voice and of not being walked over.

After each appointment with her I walked taller, maintained eye contact longer, and felt more comfortable in my skin. This new-found confidence had other life-changing effects for me too. Other kids – even some of the bullies who had traumatised me for years – started to look at me differently. No, the change didn't happen all at once, the abuse didn't stop overnight but, thanks to my developing confidence and new self-esteem, there was a noticeable shift. My teenage life, for a time, wasn't as painful.

To complement my now super-manageable, stylish hair, I started saving my pocket money to buy make-up. I spent countless evenings experimenting with eyeshadow, mascara, lipstick and foundation (a nightmare for any teenage girl, never mind a mixed-race teenage girl). I loved it. It felt good to look pretty.

And this new confidence seemed to act like a magnet to boys! Suddenly the teenage boys I secretly fancied, the ones I believed would never look twice at me, started to take notice. And then, at fifteen, I fell in love.

5

BABY, IT'S YOU

'Sabrina, the test is positive. You're pregnant.'

This isn't supposed to be happening to me. Not me, Sabrina. Not me, Mary's daughter. Not me, the future nurse. The first person in my family to go to university. Because that's been my dream forever. That's all I want to do, to be. All I have ever wanted.

Not this.

This isn't right. I can't be up the duff. I'm on the pill! I've been careful. When was I not careful? When? The volunteer at the pregnancy crisis centre giving me the life-shattering news looks at me with concern, sorrow and sadness.

Don't look at me like that. Don't pity me. I need your help, not pity.

Eve, our next-door neighbour and the only person I felt I could ask to come to this appointment with me, places her arm gently around my shoulder and rubs my arm. 'Are you OK?'

'No, I'm not. I can't believe it.' I didn't fucking expect the test to be positive. I thought I was just a few weeks late. I've been late before and I wasn't pregnant, so why am I now? What have I done wrong?

'I don't even feel pregnant,' I say to no one in particular. I just thought I'd come here and get a test to confirm that I'm not pregnant. What am I going to do?

I look up at the volunteer, who is sitting opposite me, perching on the orange-covered chair in the corner, the white pregnancy test in her hand pointing at me like a sword. 'Would you like to see for yourself?' she asks, holding it out to me.

Don't take it. If you take it, it makes it real. I look at her as if she has sentenced me to be hung, drawn and quartered. She sees it in my eyes. The fear.

'Sabrina, I don't know what you're thinking, but I can sense this might not be the news you were expecting – or maybe want.'

No shit, Sherlock.

'We at the pregnancy crisis centre are here to support you however we can, but first you will need to have the test confirmed by your doctor. They will discuss your options, should you choose to have your baby or go down another path.'

'A doctor? So, there's a chance I might not be pregnant? Until the doctor confirms it?' I reply, a glimmer of hope in my voice. She furrows her brow, looks me dead in the eye and ever so slowly says, 'There may be a very small chance that you're not pregnant. But in my experience a test that shows two blue lines as strong and as fast as yours did means that you *are* pregnant. But please, have it confirmed by your doctor. Do you understand what I'm saying?'

I hold my forehead in my hands while Eve continues to stroke my arm. 'Fuck. My mum's gonna kill me.'

I am *so* excited. It's taken until I'm seventeen years old but here I am, ticket in hand, going on my first ever foreign holiday. I get to go to an actual airport, on an actual aeroplane to mother-fucking Ibiza, baby! The party capital of Europe! And I'm going with the love of my life and the only human I want to be around 24/7. My boyfriend, Chris.

Almost everyone I know at school has been on a plane. They've come back golden and glowing, telling tales of their adventures. That's not been my life. As other kids jetted off to sunny parts of the world, we'd board an Intercity train – my sister and I got free tickets due to our dad's job working for British Rail – and head to Scotland to see our mum's family. My Scottish family also do not go on foreign holidays, so I never really felt like I was missing out. How can you miss something you've never had?

My dad hadn't missed out on foreign holidays at all. Fuck, he lived abroad for a good chunk of my young life: when my need for him burned my soul, he was off living another, more hedonistic life on – as fate would have it – the same island I am about to head to for my first holiday.

I hated my dad for choosing his Ibiza-based party life-style over us, for not being the father Sharon and I needed him to be. My resentment for him grew each year, boiling over into all aspects of my life. This led me to getting in trouble at school for fighting and being aggressive. I didn't know what to do with my rage. Whenever I used my pillow at home as a target for my anger – something the teenage magazines told me to do – I pretended it was him. I'd punch and scratch and bite the pillow, my absent father. I would speak to the pillow with hate-filled venom, low and feral: 'Where are you? You don't love me at all, do you? Why can't you be a good dad?'

He did make sporadic visits to see us, but as I got older it seemed that, for him, these visits were a form of temporary rehab as an antidote to his hedonistic lifestyle. He'd stay with me, my mum and sister and he'd try his best to revert to father mode, but the older I got the more I rebelled against it. Against him. He'd missed out on so much and had lost my respect in the process. My heart closed off and I stopped wanting him. Our relationship was broken.

It was funny that my first foreign holiday was to the same island that had captured my dad's heart in a way that I couldn't for so many years.

My senses are super heightened the entire journey. The shininess and smell of the airport. The shops displaying their multi-coloured sarongs, bikinis and hats. Each retailer wanting to entice us, the passengers, to spend our money before boarding. To capitalise on our excitement. I was at bursting point.

'Why are you smiling at me? What's so funny?' I ask Chris.

'Look at you. You're like a kid in a sweet shop. Could you *be* any more excited?'

He's been going on planes to faraway lands all his life. This is normal for him.

I keep my passport, with my ticket tucked inside, firmly in my hand. It's the first passport I have ever owned, and having it feels like a rite of passage – excuse the pun. I am a new Sabrina. A traveller. *This* is my life now. I want to travel the world! Ibiza first, then who knows where? For once, it feels there are no limits.

As we descend to land, the sea looks bluer than any water I've ever seen, aqua in places, and it shines, in luminous contrast to the white buildings, sandy beaches and coves. It's so unbelievably beautiful – and so unlike the green landscape at home. My heart skips a beat.

'We're here, Chris. We're here!'

Ibiza is all I imagined it to be, and so much more. Boat parties, pool parties, sex parties. The best nightclubs in Europe. Drugs. Alcohol. All of it. And the people – the people were the best. Back home, I didn't know anyone like this. I loved them, and for some reason, especially after I'd had a couple of drinks and gained a bit more confidence, they seemed to love me too. Me and my crazy alcohol-fuelled personality.

1995 was the year of the super club. And when it came

to Ibiza, none was bigger than Manumission. I'd read about it. Seen pictures and heard rumours about all the different rooms. It was a must-see.

'We *have* to go, Chris. We have to go to Manumission. I know that the tickets are expensive, but it'll be worth it. We can't be in Ibiza and *not* go.'

'Well, it means we'll spend the last two days of our holiday sharing two portions of lasagne but, if you're up for that, I'm in,' he replied.

I hugged him tight and kissed him all over his face in appreciation. 'It'll be amazing.'

But, thanks to drinking too much, I spend the twenty-four hours before our big night out at Manumission viciously vomiting. I'm hot, weak and utterly exhausted.

'The party girl of Ibiza is all partied out,' Chris taunts.

'Fuck off,' is the only response I feel able to give. This is my fault. It's self-inflicted. I don't know when to stop. Once I press the party button, all bets are off.

He strokes my face as we lie together on the sticky, sweat-soaked sheets. I close my eyes and begin to doze while begging my body, *Please let it pass, please make me feel better for Manumission.*

My prayers were answered.

'It's better than I ever imagined!' I shout in Chris's ear as we dance in the main atrium. I choose a spot next to a massive eight-foot speaker and the bass vibrates through my whole body. To my right is a dancer walking on stilts, in full make-up and a multi-coloured headpiece. To my left the most beautiful gay couple are kissing and gazing adoringly into each other's eyes, full of passion for each other. This is living, I thought.

Chris and I danced and kissed and laughed. There was so much possibility. We were excited for our future, whether as a couple or apart. We didn't know what the future would hold, but at that moment we didn't care. At least we had this memory to share. Forever.

'Chris, I'm pregnant.'

He was the first person I wanted to tell – the first person I had to tell. I needed to see what his reaction would be. Needed to see the whites of his eyes.

He's just sitting, motionless, on the edge of my bed in the flat I share with my mum and sister. We're only inches apart but he feels very far away.

'You're pregnant?' He just looks at me. His arms by his sides, clutching at the sheet, his knuckles getting whiter by the second. He's angry with me. He needs an answer. Needs me to make him understand how it happened. Needs an explanation, when I barely understand it myself.

'Yes, I am.'

'But you're on the pill, aren't you? I thought you couldn't get pregnant when you're on the pill.'

He's right. I take the pill! I open my bedside table drawer every morning as soon as I wake up, and I pop the pill. You can't get pregnant while on the pill, right?

'I don't know, Chris.' I stand there in front of him, vulnerable, wanting something from him which he doesn't seem able to give me. I don't even know what I need. A hug. Him telling me that everything would be alright.

But I'm lying when I say I don't know, because I cracked it this morning. I spent hours sitting in my bedroom reading and rereading the instructions that come with every pill packet I open. The ones I had ignored until twenty-four hours ago. And there in black and white it says: *If you suffer sickness (vomiting) while taking this contraceptive pill, do not continue to have sexual intercourse as this may render this method of contraception ineffective.*

The pill might not work if you're sick.

Think, Sabrina, think. What have I been doing for the last two months? I've been working, I've been out a few times, but I haven't been . . .

'Fuck!'

I had remembered. Ibiza. Before Manumission – the sickness. The sticky sheets. The only time I've been sick in the last two months.

'It says that if you're sick then it might not work. But I didn't know that, Chris,' I plead with him, my eyes starting to water. 'I didn't know. Do you remember when we were in Ibiza, and I was sick?' I'm talking at breakneck speed, tripping over my words to get it all out, to confess to him – my boyfriend of eighteen months – what I've done wrong. Because it's *my* fault.

'Even though I kept taking it, I think it weakens the pill somehow – I don't know. But that's the only time I was sick, Chris. I promise you, I take it every day. I do. You've got to believe me. I didn't think I'd get pregnant. I didn't want to get pregnant. Do you believe me?' I burst into tears because I'm scared and tired after not being able to sleep, and I really don't know what to do. This person sitting in front of me, the boy I love so much, now with his head in his hands, doesn't know what to do either. He's nineteen, I'm seventeen. Kids ourselves. *I think he might hate me.*

I sit down on the opposite side of the bed. I don't want him to feel bad for responding the way he has. It's natural, isn't it? He's in shock. Just like I was when I found out. I just need to give him time. To absorb it.

'What are you going to do?' he asks.

What am *I* going to do?

And, like clouds parting, it becomes clear that I am alone in this. He doesn't have the mental capacity to help me right now. He's dumbfounded, lost and thinking about *his* life. The impact on *him*.

I'm the only one who can decide what to do. My body, my life, my decision. But it's a decision I don't feel equipped to make.

I need to tell my mum.

My mum is on a short trip to Scotland to see Granda, who's not well. It's been two days since I told Chris, forty-eight hours of me feeling alone, unsure and scared. It's taken this long for me to pluck up courage to call my mum. I have no idea how she will respond. We've never discussed me getting pregnant. I don't want kids; I don't even really like them. My mum knows I want to be a nurse and was very practical when she knew I'd started to get it on with boys. She came with me to the doctor and helped me decide to go on the pill.

I pick up the phone, my heart beating out of my chest.

'Mum. I'm pregnant.'

The silence feels like forever, but is maybe just a few seconds. 'What? What did ye say?' she responds.

I repeat, 'I'm pregnant, Mum.'

A longer silence.

'Mum?'

In a tone I can only describe as resigned, she eventually replies, 'Well, hen. What can I say? I had you at eighteen, didn't I? What are you going to do? Does Chris know?'

Again, that question. That fucking question.

'Yeah, he knows. He's shocked. He hasn't spoken to me for a couple of days. I'm going to make an appointment with the doctor. The woman at the pregnancy crisis centre said that was the next thing I needed to do. When are you home?'

I'm not sure how I feel about the way she's taking the news. In one sense I'm pleased that she hasn't shouted at me, called me stupid, irresponsible or told me that I've brought shame on the family. But on the other hand – and I don't understand why – I do want that from her. I want her to make me properly think about the best course of action to take. I want her to mother me.

Growing up with my mum, who has so often struggled with her mental health, has been really fucking hard. To get us through the dark times, I had to assume a parental role in our family. I had to look after my mum and my little sister. That's been my life as long as I can remember: 'Make sure Mum's OK. Be good. Don't do anything to upset Mum.'

Because I've been the parent to her child for so many years, our relationship isn't like many of the mother/daughter relationships I know or see on TV. I don't feel close to her. I don't share things with her. I don't get vulnerable with her. I'm a closed book. I can't help it. It's what I've had to do.

But I know my mum loves me, and I know I need her support: right now, she's the only person I know who will stand by me through thick and thin. I can't say that confidently about anyone else in my life right now.

'Well, that positive test tells you all you need to know,' the doctor says nonchalantly as he looks down at the test. I've never liked this doctor, and he's talking to me like I'm a piece of shit. *I am not a bad person. I am not worthless. I made a mistake.*

'What's next, then?' my mum asks. It's unlike her to take the reins; that's my job.

'Sabrina, what do you want to do? Are you planning on

going through with this pregnancy, or do you know what your options are?'

I look at my mum, then back at him. 'What are my options?' I ask meekly.

'Well, quite simply, young lady, you can carry on with this pregnancy. If you do that, I would refer you to our practice midwife. Or there's termination of the pregnancy – if you decide on that, I'd refer you to another unit. Or you might want to explore other avenues, such as adoption.'

'I'm not giving my baby away!' I say with such force that I surprise myself. My voice doesn't sound like my own; I sound possessed. He stares, my mum stares. My hands are trembling, I'm getting hot, my skin is starting to itch.

'No one is going to make you give your baby away, Sabrina. This is your decision. Your life. Your future,' he responds. There's more care in his voice now. Less judgement.

I'm embarrassed by my outburst and shocked by the words I used – 'my baby'. By calling it that instead of 'the pregnancy', something has happened. Something funda-mental in this decision-making process.

Love. Love for *my baby* has happened.

'So you're going to keep the baby?' my mum probes as we sit across from each other in the coffee shop afterwards.

'Yeah, I think so,' I lie. I know I'm going to keep it. 'It's no one's fault but my own that I'm in this position, and it's my responsibility to deal with it.' My calm, matter-of-fact tone shocks me. *Who even am I?* 'I'll talk to Chris about it later, but nothing he says is going to make me change my mind. If he wants to stand by me, great. If he doesn't, that's his decision. It was never my plan to have a baby at eighteen, but if this is the plan for me, then I'll live with it.'

'OK. Well, you know I'm here for you, whatever.'

And I did.

The weeks after my doctor's appointment were hard. My decision to keep my baby was challenged by adults and friends who believed that my decision would negatively impact on them. They acted as if I had made the decision without enough consideration of what the future might hold. That I had no idea what life as a teenage mother with a handful of GCSEs to her name would be like. All the old tropes were rolled out for me: *Do you know how hard having a child is? You'll ruin your life. You'll never amount to anything. You'll be living off the state. You're so young! It's kids having kids. Yet another statistic.*

Some of these things were said to my face but most were behind my back, for other people to report back to me. Every single one stung me.

And Chris is just about to go off to university. That really got to me. What they really meant was that my decision to keep *our* baby would make it difficult for him to fulfil *his* dream of going to university. Everyone said that. It was often the first thing they said, before they asked me about anything else. How will *his* life, *his* dreams be impacted? I was an afterthought. In their eyes, I had made my bed and had to lie in it.

The only person who didn't feel I should get rid of my baby was my mum. She knew, maybe even better than I did, that I could cope. I had cared for her when she needed me, hadn't I? I had played mother to her. My mum's resolute support of my decision, of sharing her lived experience of being a teenage mum, and her single-minded care for the welfare of me and my baby, made me feel confident that I could do it. I could be a mum, because she had.

'Well, I was a teenager when I had you,' she'd say. 'And you turned out alright, didn't you?'

While there were plenty of times that I felt far from alright, she was always there, ready to help.

He's leaving. This is really happening. He's going to university 100 miles away and I'm going to be on my own in this. Yes, he'll ring me and he'll come back when he gets the chance, but to all intents and purposes I will be a single, pregnant teenager. He'll be living the life of a young man in a university town doing whatever he wants. I have to trust him, I know I do, but I'm jealous and it hurts to see him go.

I know this is what we discussed. This is what he wants to do – what he needs to do. I have given him my blessing, told him I'll be OK, and enabled him to continue to pursue his dream. I would never stand in the way of him getting his degree. I don't want to stop him doing the thing he's always dreamed of.

I've made an effort to be positive about it all, but I don't want him to leave me. I want him to love me so much that he finds another way. A way that means he can be here with me when I feel the baby's first kick, to hold my hair while I'm being sick, to come to my first midwife appointment. And what about my dream of being a nurse? I wanted to be the first person in my family to go to university, to get a degree, to show them all that I'm good enough to do those things. That I'm smart enough. That there's more to me. It's almost unbearable to think of that life. The one I will never have.

All people see now is a seventeen-year-old girl who's up the duff and has thrown her life away because of a stupid, stubborn decision.

'Hey, what's wrong? We're all going to miss him, aren't we?' says Chris's mum as she catches a glimpse of my tears in the rear-view mirror. I smile weakly and quickly wipe my face. Since Chris has been in my life so has his mum, Amanda. A quiet, kind woman who worships the ground that Christopher and his brother walk on. If she ever thought that I shouldn't keep the baby then she's played a blinder in hiding it from me, because all I've ever felt from her is love and support. And I just know she's going to be the most amazing nanny.

I don't want him to see I'm upset. This is *his* experience, and I shouldn't ruin it. She doesn't understand that I'm crying for so much more. Yes, I'm crying because he's leaving me, but I'm also crying because of what I've given up. My dreams. My experiences. My what could have been.

We arrive at his new home just outside Southampton. He couldn't get student digs so his mum helped him find a room with a couple she knows who live nearby. I make polite conversation with his female host as we unpack the car. She's pregnant, too – a few months ahead of me, judging by her bump – and we compare notes on morning sickness and cravings. She seems so friendly. I think he'll be happy here. I hope he will be, anyway.

As I stand there in his little room, which now it's full of his things has already started to smell of him – the smell I love – I feel bereft. I don't want to do this alone. I don't want to go to midwife appointments alone. I want him with me. That's how it's supposed to be. We're supposed to be together.

He gets up from the bed, arms outstretched, and looks down at me. 'Give me a hug,' he says. I bury my face in his chest, encircling my arms around his waist.

'I don't want to leave you,' I sob. 'I don't want to go back home. You're so far away. Who am I going to talk to? I'm going to be so alone.'

Does he not know that he is my world? I love him so much, it hurts. That's not just a throwaway comment; my love for him actually *hurts* me. I have willingly buried my immediate needs to make this experience – his higher education experience – as normal for him as possible. My need to feel loved has been cast aside for his to be fulfilled.

I can't even blame him. It feels that this love – this

self-sacrifice – is my destiny. It's the only way I know how to love or to be loved. With my mother, my absent father, those whom I choose to love – or whom it is my duty to love – their needs must always come before mine. I have always, and must always, take care of their needs first. Mine must never be the priority. My lived experience has shown that, when I put myself first, bad things happen. Fathers leave. Mothers struggle to cope. Things get very bad.

We stand there, holding tight, for minutes, knowing that this is it, that we've got to part and get on with our new separate lives.

'I have to go.'

When his mum starts the car, he leans in through the open window, placing a gentle kiss on her cheek.

'Get some food inside you, and some rest. Everything will be fine. We'll look after her,' she says to him. I raise a smile, swallowing back tears. I can't speak. He stands aside and we start moving. *Don't look back.* I keep my gaze focused on the road ahead.

The sonographer moves the scanning device over my belly and I start to worry.

'Is everything OK?'

'Sabrina, I think you may have drunk a bit too much water. You'll need to go and empty your bladder a little – but not completely. There's a toilet just here. Let me help you off the bed.'

I'm so embarrassed. She's being nice but I bet she thinks I'm stupid. *Stupid teenage mum.*

'Oh. Oh, right. OK.' I actually think I might wee myself after her prodding me. *Sabrina, don't piss yourself, for God's sake!* The sonographer lends me her arm and I get off the bed, open the door and waddle to the toilet.

How was I to know how much water to drink? It said on the letter that I had to drink a litre of water for the sonographer to see the baby on the screen. So I drank that and a bit more, you know, to be on the safe side.

'How do I know how much to let out?' I ask my mum, who has accompanied me to the loo.

'I don't know, hen, probably about half,' she says.

'Yeah, but I don't know what half is. I'm about to piss myself and if I start peeing I might not be able to stop. I don't know if my fanny has the strength to cease mid-flow.'

She bursts out laughing.

'For God's sake, don't make me laugh,' I shout as I hurry into the cubicle. Pants down, bum on seat. 'Ahhhhhh, that feels good.'

'Where are you?' I text him, for the fifth time, from the loo. He promised he'd be here. He left home early this morning to beat the traffic.

'He'd better not miss this,' I say to my mum as I wash my hands.

'Does he know what time it is?'

'Yes, Mum, I've told him loads of times.'

I'm twenty weeks pregnant, and this is the scan to show us how the baby is doing. Is it developing normally? Is it the right shape and size? Does it have ten fingers and toes? We're not going to find out the sex. That doesn't matter to us. All that matters is that it's OK.

But what if it's not? What if something is wrong and he's not here to hear the news? I suppose it would be just another thing in this pregnancy that I have to go through on my own.

But he's there when we go back into the sonographer's room. He looks stressed.

'You alright?' he says as he falls into line behind me.

'Where the hell have you been?' I whisper, angry.

'Traffic was shit and then I couldn't find anywhere to park. Sorry.'

'Just assume the position you were in, Sabrina. That's it, perfect,' the sonographer says. 'You might feel some pressure on your bladder, which will be uncomfortable due to the water you have drunk, but not as bad as before.' She winks. 'I just need to get this instrument in the right position to take photos of your baby.'

My heart is beating faster. All eyes are on the screen. We're waiting, waiting to see something, anything. As I feel her move the scanner over my belly – over the top, the sides, pressing – I feel the urge to wee again.

'Can you see it? Is my baby OK?'

'Hold on there a second, Sabrina. I'm sure we'll— Oh, there it is.'

She points to a small area on the screen. I spot a tiny, almost invisible, circle contract and release. *Contract, release, contract, release.*

'That's your baby's heart, Sabrina.' As she says it, she turns up the volume of the TV and the room is filled with a loud, fast, beat. *Do dum, do dum, do dum.*

'That's my baby's heartbeat?' I say, amazed at its strength. A real-life heartbeat inside me that's not mine. I can't stop looking at the little circle. 'Is it supposed to be that fast? Is that normal?'

'Yes, it's completely normal,' she replies as she continues to scan my belly.

I feel an overwhelming love and immense relief that my baby's alive. Of course I have felt flutters, and my midwife told me these sensations are the baby moving, but to me they have felt like trapped wind. I'm a very windy person, I'm not ashamed to say. But now I know for sure that I'm holding more than just wind. There's a life in there.

'There's a foot. Oh, and baby is crossing its legs, looking very comfortable in there. Can you see?' She points to what, at first, looks like fog, but then as she draws her finger against the outline, I see it.

'It's a foot. Look, Chris.'

He's looking at the screen too, a look of bewilderment on his face. 'Yeah, I can see.'

I look at the screen. My baby. It has two feet, two legs, a head, two arms. I have made a baby. 'Is it OK? Is it normal?'

'Yes, Sabrina. Your baby is measuring well for dates. I see nothing untoward in its development.' As she looks at the screen, she asks us whether we want to know the sex.

'No.' My quick reply. 'I want something to look forward to at the end of the labour!'

She, my mum and Chris laugh.

'It's true. After what I might have to go through, I want a nice surprise.'

Chris helps me into a sitting position on the bed and the sonographer hands us six printed images of our baby. 'Something to cherish until you get to meet him or her in twenty weeks' time.'

As I sit in the driver's seat of the car alone – Chris has gone to find his car and my mum has walked into town for groceries – I stroke the pictures. The human I have created that everyone around me, bar my mum, told me was a mistake to keep. The thing that will ruin my life. The baby that will make me just another statistic. But right now I don't feel like a statistic, a failure or less than anyone else. I feel like a fucking queen. I feel proud of me, of my body and of my little bump.

I trace my finger around the outline of its body, its button nose, its tiny feet and fingers, stroking my belly. 'We'll be OK, baby. I'll keep you safe, I promise.' And then, as if my bump has understood, I get a kick in response. 'Mumma loves you.'

'I've got the shits,' I say bluntly. 'Not only are my tits all veiny and melon-like, not only are my nipples black, not only have

I got angry red stretch marks all over my body, but now – to top it all off – I have the shits too.'

I am eighteen years and almost two months old. I am a big, fat, ugly mess. My mum has mentioned, one time too many, how she actually *lost weight* when she was pregnant with me. For a while, I thought this might be genetic, but it clearly is not! I have gained 3 stone.

'Do you still fancy me?' I ask Chris.

He doesn't even look up at me as he replies, 'Yeah, course.'

Fucking liar. 'I'm going to bed. I can't take this much longer, Chris. It's alright for you.'

He looks up but my expression signals to him that it's best he doesn't respond.

I pull down my pants, sit on the toilet seat, and then I see it. The red, jelly-like mucous. I prod it with my finger. It's not like anything I've seen before. And the red? That's blood, and blood in pregnancy is not a good sign.

'Chris!' I shout. 'Chris, come here. Come now. Something has happened.'

He walks to the bathroom, looks down at my pants then back at me. 'What's that?' he says.

'I dunno. I think it might be a show. But I dunno. I've never seen one in real life.'

We both look.

'Well, what do we do?'

'I'll call the maternity hospital,' I reply.

As I communicate the texture and appearance of the

mucous to the midwife on the phone, she confirms I have potentially had a show.

'Oh, right. What happens now?' I ask.

'Well, it could still be some time until labour is established. What I'd recommend is to go back to bed, get some sleep and see if things progress. We don't need you to come here until you're having regular contractions, about three to four minutes apart.'

I put down the phone and relay the information to Chris. 'She said to go back to bed as it might be ages until I go into proper labour.'

He seems relieved. 'Well, let's get some kip then.'

Five hours later, another contraction rages through my body, feeling like it's ripping me apart from the inside out. Five hours since the midwife told me it might be some time until labour is established. She lied. Because my contractions are now one minute apart, and I can't cope. I'm not in control of what's happening to me, and I'm scared.

When we arrived at the hospital a few hours ago, when the contractions became too agonising to handle at home, Sandy – a specialist midwife who works with teenage mothers and has been caring for me since my first trimester – was waiting for me. My mum was there too, Chris having called her with instructions, from me, to 'get on her bloody moped and meet us pronto at the maternity unit. This baby is coming'. It feels like so long ago, that earlier stage when the pain felt unmanageable. Little did I know just how much worse it would become, the excruciatingly painful process of bringing life into the world.

'Mum. Help me. Please help me. I can't do it.' I look up at her, pleading. 'Please help me.' I have her hand in a vice grip and, when each contraction comes, I squeeze hard. It's hurting her, I can see, but she doesn't say a thing. Chris, on my left, looks very pale, like he might be sick. But I don't care about that because *my* pain, the rip-roaring tidal wave of each contraction, is worse than anything I have ever felt before. As each one takes hold and squeezes the life – this baby – out of me, I scream.

'Please make it stop,' I beg.

They give me gas and air, but it makes me vomit. They try me on a TENS machine, but it gives me no relief, so I pull it off in frustration.

'Pethidine is all we have left to offer you, Sabrina. If you want anything stronger, you'll have to be transferred by ambulance to the Royal Hospital. That ambulance ride, at this stage of labour, will not be comfortable at all. You could even end up delivering your baby en route.'

'Give me whatever you have. Please, just make the pain go away. I can't take it,' I cry to Sandy.

'I need you to know that the effects of the pethidine can transfer to the baby. It might slow down your labour, which may lead to complications meaning you'll need to be transferred anyway.'

I'm at the point where I don't care about the risks; I just need to escape this torture. My only concern is me. 'I'll take the risk. Give me the shot.'

Pethidine is the most wonderful thing. Within minutes of having the injection, all the pain is numbed. Yes, I'm aware that I'm having contractions, but they're manageable. For the first time in what seems like eternity, I feel comfortable enough to sleep. With my screams silenced, the energy in the room calms. I mellow and my tense, contraction-ravaged body starts to relax.

Teetering between reality and a dream state, I feel a warmth between my legs, but I say nothing. I just want to sleep. To savour the peace. To get a few hours' rest. When Sandy asks to examine me half an hour later, I don't want to play ball.

'Sabrina, I just need you to turn around so I can examine you. To see whether you have dilated any more.'

'Can't I just sleep? Please, I just want to sleep.' My plea seems to fall on deaf ears, and she and my mum turn me onto my back.

When she pulls up the sheet, Sandy is greeted by blood. A lot of blood. Too much blood. My baby's head has crowned – and I'm too drugged up and off my tits to realise it.

'So *that* was the warm feeling,' I said to myself in my head, or out loud.

In seconds the whole room goes into red alert. I mean, Sandy lurched across me to literally press the big 'red alert' button directly above my head.

'Have you felt pressure, Sabrina? For how long? Do you want to push?'

Too many questions, all relayed quickly, directly to me.

'I dunno. Maybe.'

Two more midwifes enter the room. One of them pulls a big-wheeled contraption with a tiny lamp at the top and a small bed underneath. The other hands my midwife a green parcel which, when she opens it, contains a variety of shiny metal medical tools – scary-looking equipment that shocks the life out of me and ruins my mellow pethidine high.

'We need to get you delivered, fast. Do you understand? You need to listen to me very carefully.'

I nod. It has all got very serious, very tense, all of a sudden.

'When you feel an urge to push, I want you to bear down, chin to chest, and push down, push your baby out. Keep going until you feel the contraction pass or I tell you to stop. Is that clear?'

I nod and take Chris's and my mum's hands in mine. 'I can feel one coming.'

'OK, Sabrina, start pushing now . . .'

It takes half an hour. Half an hour of feeling like my body is going to split in half, of feeling like I can't open any further. Every push weakens me and zaps all my energy reserves. 'I don't have anything left to give,' I cry.

Then Sandy tells me I can do it in one more big push.

I put my chin to my chest and roar the life I created out of me. My baby.

My baby girl.

Sandy lifts her onto my chest. A little thing. A small, wet, wrinkled human being. My baby. The most precious thing I have ever seen.

I stroke her warm, downy back, hold her up to my face and inhale her scent. Her black hair is stuck in clumps to her head. I gently run my finger across her cheek and down her button nose, just like I have done to her scan photo so many times.

'Hello, Rhiannon,' I whisper. 'I'm your mummy.' I place my finger inside her tiny hand and instantly she clamps hers around it. 'You're so strong,' I say to her.

'So is her mummy,' says Sandy. I look up. Chris is in tears, and so's my mum. All for her, for us – the teenage mum who wouldn't do what they told her and her baby girl.

People might have classed us as 'another statistic', but Rhiannon was my proudest achievement to date. I could feel a fire burning inside me, spitting sparks that transformed into a series of promises, words of intent from the deepest parts of my soul.

'I love you more than anything in the world. There is nothing I won't do to provide for you, my baby. I'll make you proud, I promise. We'll show them all.'

Eighteen months later, on Christmas Eve 1997, Chris and

I welcomed our second child, a son, Brandon. My beautiful, brown-skinned baby boy and the most precious addition to our young family. Brandon was planned because I wanted our children to be close in age – and, since I was a stay-at-home mum at that time, I thought that if Chris and I were only going have two kids, then I might as well get both out of the way while I was young. I felt so lucky. Blessed to have two healthy children, a boyfriend who loved me and who was a great, totally present dad – something I never had. It felt like we had given our kids the greatest gift of all: a complete family unit. And now that Chris had graduated from university, we could be a proper family. Yep, we'd bloody well showed them all!

For two years, as we settled into family life and Chris secured his first post-university job, I felt that all the sacrifices I had made had been worthwhile. People were eating their words. We'd made it through the hardest bits. It was plain sailing now.

But I was wrong.

When the millennium celebrations rang in a new decade, the toll of the bells – unbeknownst to me – signalled changes ahead that would alter the course of my life. The life I had created and cherished.

As a kid, I could never fully experience happy times. I remember it so clearly. Every single time something good happened to me – or to us as a family – I would wait in crippling fear for the repercussions. For the bad thing.

'Don't get too happy, a bad thing is coming,' I would say

to myself, over and over. This thought process stole happiness from me so many times, so that I never experienced true joy in anything. As a child I never had the words to explain that feeling – those heart flutters, the fear of the unknown, the sadness. I now know it is anxiety.

In 2000 something changed. For me, it started with the old familiar feeling, a gut-wrenching sensation – almost physical in nature – that a bad thing is coming. I could almost taste it, the feeling was so strong. *A bad thing is coming, Sabrina. Get ready. It's coming.*

Something between Chris and me wasn't right. The jigsaw puzzle pieces of our life weren't fitting together as smoothly as they once did. I didn't know why or what I had done wrong. Some days I felt like I was pushing water uphill in my efforts to ignore the voice in my head that said bad things about me, about him, about the world we inhabited.

He doesn't love me any more.

I tried, oh my God I tried, to ignore the bad feeling. I tried to numb the ugly thoughts by staying busy, by being a good mum, but as months passed the feeling became stronger. I was increasingly fearful for myself and for my little family, my universe, that was so precious to me.

And then, after months of anguish, it finally happened: the conversation between us. I'll admit that I forced it, because I couldn't take another day of self-loathing, of not feeling like I was enough. So, through my tears and vociferous demands for the truth, I got it.

He felt too young to settle down. With me. Too young to settle down *with me*.

And with that my world imploded.My heart – and all my dreams for our future – broke that day. Yet again I wasn't enough for a man. This time it was the father of my own children; before that, it had been my dad. Chris did agree to try again – I made him, 'for the kids' – for a few months. But once he felt that the grass was greener on the other side, my attempts to make him see us as his future were futile.

Feeling totally and utterly broken, and not knowing how to deal with the pain I felt, I also sought comfort in the arms of another man. But he was nothing compared to Chris. My love.

Chris left me in late summer 2000. I say he left me because he made it perfectly clear, when he packed his things, that it was me he didn't want to be with any more. He adored his children and would always want to spend time with them, but not me. Not Sabrina.

They were dark months. After he left me, I felt hopeless. Totally devoid of any form of positivity. When I saw him, when he came to pick up the children, I'd pretend I was OK. But I wasn't. He and my babies would leave me waving and smiling at them as they walked away, and when they were out of sight I'd crumble. Dropping to the floor, my arms hugging my knees, rocking back and forth, I'd sob, 'Please love me, too.'

I found solace at the bottom of a wine glass. Nothing else

took the pain away. And as I sipped my wine and slipped into the chasm of unconsciousness, I often thought of my mum, for it felt as if my life was becoming a carbon copy of hers. In my teenage years I would angrily shout at her, 'I'll never ever be like you!' Now, sitting here, I understood it. Her pain. To love so completely, to sacrifice so much, then to have that love rejected – it's brutal. It's life-changing. And I had no idea just how much things were about to change.

6

A NEW DIRECTION

'She said that a four-year-old could write better than me?' I ask, mortified, not wanting to believe what I am hearing.

Marion, the vocational qualification tutor from the local college, looks sympathetically at me.

I'm on the brink of tears. 'I know I've got a lot to learn, Marion. For God's sake, I haven't had a job since I worked on the checkouts at Tesco when I was pregnant with my first child. But am I really that bad at writing?'

I haven't done a lot of professional administration over the past three and a half years because I've been at home looking after my two young children. But now my boyfriend has left me and his job, which was supposed to provide for all of us, is of no use to me, so I have to get a job. I can't – won't – rely on state handouts. I want *more* for my children, more for their lives. Surely, even though I haven't been employed for three years, I will have something of value to offer an employer?

It turns out that I do. I have an unmatched enthusiasm and passion to be something, after promising my newborn child that 'we'd show them'. That we'd be so much more than anyone else labelled us. My new employer sees my chutzpah, they say, and it bags me this job as an administration assistant paying £6,000 per annum. It wasn't my ability to string a sentence together that got me the job, apparently.

'I'm so embarrassed,' I say to Marion, feeling myself flush. 'I'm trying my best and spending ages checking my work before I submit it. I know I – I mean, my *work* is not good enough for them, I can sense it, but I'm doing all I can to be better.'

She looks at me, places her warm hand on my forearm and pats me, just as you would a pet dog. She means to comfort me. 'Sabrina, I know you're trying. I've reviewed your work and I believe their comments are overly critical. Yes, your writing could be better, but to compare your comprehension to a pre-schooler does you a disservice.'

I blink back the tears I feel gathering because I don't want her to feel uncomfortable. I have to remain professional. *Don't you dare cry.* 'Marion, will you explain to me what's wrong with this section?' I ask, pointing to a paragraph in the document I'm working on. 'I don't know what I'm doing wrong.'

I know I need help. Although it's excruciatingly hard for me to ask, I think Marion honestly wants to assist me in proving my employers wrong. She gives my forearm a squeeze as she pushes her glasses up her nose. 'Of course. Let's go back to basics.'

After breaking up with Chris, I decided to close myself off emotionally to all but my children. I didn't want to fall in love again. My sole focus was them; well, them and my job. Caring for them and bettering myself professionally to make a new life for us was my top priority.

That was, until they went to see their father. I had to fill this dreaded time as best I could to numb the heartbreak I felt. I had been ignoring it by keeping busy. I distracted myself in two ways. First, by drinking alone or with friends, and second, with men – or one man. Neil.

I remember the first time I saw him. It was during the summer, when my relationship was nearing its end. He was captain of my best friend's boyfriend's football team and I spotted him at an end-of-season football presentation. He had dark hair and brown eyes. My type. I thought his awkwardness when accepting a trophy was cute. My interest was piqued.

A few months later, single and – so my friends said – ready to mingle, one evening I found myself in the clutches of an overly familiar man in a town centre pub. Looking for an escape route, I clocked Neil and quickly ducked out of the letch's embrace and into Neil's.

'I need you to protect me from that dude over there. Pretend we're together or something. Help me shake him off.'

He obliged. He did what any red-blooded male who fancied a woman would do. He kissed me.

It was a nice kiss. Unexpected. I felt the spark, the chemistry between us. This could be just what I need, I thought. I'd heard from friends that Neil was single, a ladies' man; definitely not long-term boyfriend material. If I was looking for a few months of fun, knock myself out, they said. But no more than that.

They couldn't have been more wrong.

Following that first kiss, Neil only had eyes for me. That first kiss led to a date three days later. He was such a welcome distraction: he sent me humorous text messages and was relaxed and laid-back, but also kind of obsessed with me. He made me feel amazing. My confidence grew every time we met. He was fun, attractive and just what I needed.

'Until New Year,' was what I told my best friend Jen. 'I'm having fun with him until New Year and then that'll be it.'

I knew Neil was falling for me, and quickly. No matter how distant I was emotionally, it didn't seem to faze him. I didn't want him to fall in love with me. I didn't want the burden of breaking his heart when I ended it. I knew that pain, and I didn't want to inflict it on someone I liked. Someone who, in a few short months, had given me so much.

But I had to end it at New Year. 2001 had to be a fresh start for me and the kids. Just me and them.

Neil had secured us some tickets for a New Year's Eve ball. I hadn't told anyone that I intended to let things fizzle out, that my heart was not yet healed, that I intended to move on with my life, without him. My plan was to do it the week after. I didn't want to ruin his night, or mine.

I was standing at the bar, looking around, when I witnessed an interaction that changed things. It unlocked something inside me. I saw him across the room, in lively conversation with his friends, throwing his head back in laughter, an arm draped around the shoulders of the man next to him. Exuding confidence. Oozing sex appeal. And I wasn't the only one who noticed.

They came in from the right, like lionesses stalking prey. Two women, champagne glasses in hand and lip-gloss smiles, breaking into the circle of men. *What is this?* I thought. Quickly followed by, *not him too.*

It was like a movie. Everyone else in the room blurred out and I saw only him. Some invisible thread must have pulled at him, because he looked up, looking for something. Until he found it: me. He smiled, and it was a smile that spoke a thousand words. He left the women and his friends and came over to me.

'Hello, are you OK?' he said, smiling adoringly at me.

'I am now,' I replied.

And, for the first time in a while, I did feel OK. In fact, I felt better than I had done in some time. The time I spent with Neil had a noticeable impact on my drinking too – in a good way, a healthy way. Because when I was with him – and even when I was not with him – he made me feel special, beautiful and strong. He said that one of the things that attracted him to me was my independence, my focus.

'You don't need anyone, yet you choose to spend time with me. I like that,' he'd say. And that feeling of being valued, of feeling love, was one I didn't want to forget, didn't want to anaesthetise myself from. I didn't need to lean on the crutch of alcohol to have my needs met. I felt amazing.

And with that, I made the decision to give our relationship a chance. I opened my heart a little. Allowing myself to accept love again was hard for me, especially in the early days. It was hard for him too, knowing that he came after my children and my job. But his love for me, from the start, was strong enough for both of us. Within nine months of our first kiss, we had fallen in love. This was enough to convince me to buy our first house together.

I have never forgotten the comment my first employer made about my literacy. It stayed with me throughout my career in public relations and still, to this day, it's a stick I use to beat myself with. *Why would anyone want to read anything you write? You're illiterate!*

Why is it always so much easier to remember negative events than positive events in your life? I admit, it's a constant struggle for me to remember the good stuff, and that's why I have created a treasure trove of people, places and things to remind myself of my awesomeness. I try to spend quality time with people who lift me up and, just by being in their aura, nourish my soul. I go on early morning runs to the top of local viewpoints, breakfast in my backpack, to watch the sunrise and I'll remind myself that *even in the dark times, the light always comes.* And, from my memory box, I like to look at a tattered drawing of a little girl's mum winning a race in the Sahara Desert. These are some of the tools I use to keep my head above water when the black dog of depression comes sniffing.

It also helps a lot when you have a soulmate. Neil tells me every day how amazing he thinks I am. Over the years, during my depressive episodes, this powerhouse of a human reminds me who I am and brings me back to the light.

My first employer's opinion of my literacy was communicated to me as an area of weakness when new employers asked for a reference. I spent years feeling branded, and that invisible-to-all-but-me mark has stayed with me. My perceived weakness, something that I studiously continued to work on throughout my career in PR because I *wanted* to be better, became a whip for all employers to beat me with. To put me back in my place. To not let me get ahead of myself.

In late 2003 I felt ripped apart because, on the one hand, I was singlehandedly winning massive clients thanks to my passion and enthusiasm, but on the other hand I was being lambasted for not being able to write what *they* believed to be a strong enough press release. I was getting results, and the companies I worked with had no complaints about my work, but I felt that I was being held back and side-lined for promotion. No matter how hard I tried, I could progress no further.

In 2004, buoyed by Neil's love and support – by then he was my fiancé – I was ready to take the leap to self-employment. The opportunity to earn my monthly salary in just four days was too good to ignore. I'd had enough of the carrot-dangling and was tired of jumping through hoops to please people who didn't care about me, my career, or my well-being. I wanted more than they could give me, so I jumped ship four months before our wedding, and made the decision to play by my own rules. I would focus on my strengths and address my weaknesses in a manner that felt right for me. On my terms. I would shoot for the stars by branching out on my own.

Some people might say that starting a business four months before getting married is stupid. But for me, it made sense. Marrying Neil signified a new phase of my life; after the heartbreak of 2000, I was finally able to be vulnerable with another man, and I loved and appreciated him for the support he had given me.

Together we agreed that my earning capacity – if all went to plan – was much more than his, so we decided that he would look after the home and the children during the day – kids he had grown to love as his own – leaving me to focus on setting up and building the business. Many people, including members of our families, were surprised at our decision and asked Neil repeatedly if he was OK with it. He never wavered in his response.

'Of course I am. We're a team. Me being at home allows Sabrina to focus on what she needs to do to build the business and provide for us. Why would I not be OK with that?'

They would be silent for a moment, nod, then move on to the next topic of conversation. I would look at Neil with so much respect, admiration and love, knowing that he was so special.

From Day 1 Neil was willing to give up so much for me: his lady-loving ways, his single lifestyle and even – when I agreed in 2001 to give our relationship a proper try – having his own children. I was clear with him from the start that Rhiannon and Brandon were all I needed, and I wasn't planning on having more children.

'If you want to be with me, with us, then you have to be happy with this. With us being enough.'

He said he was. He loved me. He loved my children. We were enough.

People use the word 'emasculation' a lot, especially when referring to a relationship that includes a strong woman who gets shit done. They look at the man and say 'he didn't have a choice – she told him what to do.' I call this bullshit. Comments like this are made with the sole purpose of negating women, to cast doubt over their relationship, to put a woman back in her box. I have never, and will never, take this kind of thing lying down.

Neil always had a choice. He chose – and continues to choose – me. He has always been my number-one cheer-leader, and vice versa. Of course, our relationship has had its ups and downs – more my fault than his – but his love and belief in me have never waned. Because, like we always say, we're a team. When one of us succeeds, we both do. When one of us bleeds, we both do. Our love only gets stronger, because we are equals.

And for the naysayers, any person who chooses to support their partner to be the best version of themselves is far from emasculated. They are the most self-assured, confident people out there. Neil and I both know that I couldn't do it alone.

I knew from the moment I won my first client that I had the sales skills I needed to build a great business. Even before I left pitch meetings, prospective clients would be falling over themselves to sign on the dotted line. In those early days of running my business, it felt like everything I touched turned to gold.

I loved the buzz of working in PR. The feeling of excitement I would always get when I saw a client of mine in a newspaper, on TV or radio. It was like a drug. It felt amazing to know that my nose for a good story, combined with the relationships I had developed with journalists or editors, had resulted in coverage – and ultimately a higher profile and better sales – for my clients. I lived for that hit and was fuelled by the need for more: more success, more recognition and more income.

I fast became 'one to watch' and was included on 'top 30 aged under 30' lists of businesspeople. I loved every minute of it.

I had long dreamed of winning one industry award: Young Communicator of the Year. I had been shortlisted for the award while I was in my last role, but I didn't win and was absolutely gutted. My confidence knocked, I promised myself that, should I go for the award again, my portfolio would be unbeatable.

Two years after I launched my business, I decided to put myself forward. Something inside me needed that award, that recognition from my peers: a physical award that I could hold in my hands that told me I was one of the best. That I was good enough. I needed that award to show people who said I was illiterate that I could still succeed. I needed it as a 'fuck you' to them.

The awards ceremony was held early in 2006. As Neil and I sat in the massive, glitzy conference room, what no one else there knew was that I was three months pregnant. Yes, I had mellowed. I'd changed my mind about having more children. Why? Because of Neil. Because his love and support, and his love and protection for his stepchildren, showed me that he deserved to have his own biological children too. And I wanted to give them to him. A baby would be the ultimate gift I could give this man. When we decided to try, I fell pregnant within a month. It was meant to be.

At the ceremony, I shook with nerves. Neil and I were surrounded by the great and the good of the PR industry – people with much more experience than me. People who had been university educated. I couldn't help thinking that I didn't belong there.

Neil sensed my anxiety. 'Relax. Enjoy this. You've earned the right to be here,' he said, taking my hand. I mustered the best smile I could and took a deep breath.

Young Communicator was the penultimate award of the night. It was one of the bigger awards, and the organisers wanted the tension to build – it certainly was in me. After what felt like a lifetime, the lights dimmed and the compère – a well-known comedian – took to the stage to announce the finalists and winners.

I couldn't look up, so I focused on the pattern on my black chiffon skirt. My heart was hammering as my name was announced, along with the four other finalists.

Oh my God. This is it. Please, give me this. Please.

Under the table, Neil grabbed my hand. He knew how important this was to me. 'It'll be OK, Bumblebee. You're the best.'

I closed my eyes and slowly breathed in.

'And the winner is . . .'

Time stopped.

'Sabrina Pace-Humphreys, Storm PR.'

Neil was already up, punching the air. He threw his arms around me, lifting me up, and I could hear the whole conference room swoon. They could all see it: Neil's pride in me, the love we share, the team we are.

Everyone clapped. Old colleagues and others who knew me whooped in celebration. I felt honoured – recognised by my peers for my determination to be the best. The sacrifices I had chosen to make had been worth it, and to share the moment with my soulmate was a dream.

That award heralded the start of a long, prosperous stint for me and my business. It was called Storm PR until March 2006, when I rebranded as Trailblazer PR. My confidence after winning that award pushed me to work even harder for a life that I believed would make me happy, fulfilled and content.

In August 2006 we welcomed our daughter Bo. I worked up until the day she was born, even replying to emails in the car on the way to the maternity unit, such was my dedication to building my business and making sure my clients had the very best service. When other pregnant women I knew were attending pre-natal classes, I was presenting to board members. When they were having coffee with their family and friends, I was grabbing a sandwich and eating it alone in the car park of a motorway service station. These were my choices. When I felt emotional about what I was missing, I would remind myself firmly that no one was forcing me to work this hard.

This is on you. Pull up your big girl pants.

But even so, I regularly felt a lack of connection to my growing body, sometimes even to the human growing inside me.

I went back to full-time work two weeks after I had given birth to my beautiful baby girl. The moment I held her, my worries about whether I would have enough love to give another child dissipated. Seeing her older sister and brother with her was everything to me. They adored her. Cradled her. Sang to her. She was the invisible glue bonding us all forever.

Leaving our little family unit two weeks after Bo was born was horrible, but I had to go back to work. I had staff to manage, clients to keep happy, and – now – another mouth to feed. But I hated work now. Breastfeeding was a chore, something to endure. It's no fun sitting in a dark, cold meeting room, hand-expressing milk from your swollen boobs, knowing that your baby – the baby who wants to feed from you, not a bottle – is at home.

But I pushed down my feelings. I had to, to survive. To continue working. I had to forget about being a stay-at-home mum. After all, that wasn't the life I had chosen. I chose this. Being a businesswoman was my choice, so I had to suck it up.

I never wanted to appear weak or out of control. I never wanted to ask for help, but three years later, in November 2009 I became pregnant with my fourth child. I started to feel as if I was losing my grip. Dark thoughts – feelings that something bad was going to happen – got even darker and more frequent. These episodes affected me and everyone around me. I'd fly off the handle, going from nought to one hundred in the blink of an eye. I'd either be in a blind rage or bursting into tears. I was a Jekyll and Hyde. I was looking for something, someone, to blame. I blamed my hormones, saying that the pregnancy – this baby – was making me crazy. Even my own husband and children looked at me like I was someone they didn't know.

'Babe, you need to relax,' Neil would say.

'How can I relax?' I'd snap back. 'If I relax, it all goes wrong. It always does.'

That's what my mind told me. *Don't lose control, don't let go.*

My business was five years old. I had staff. I had clients. I had kids. A house. A husband. I had all I could want. So why wasn't I happy? Why was I always so fucking difficult to please? People needed me, so I had to maintain control, or at least pretend that everything was under control. On top of this, I developed symphysis pubis disorder (SPD), which left me in horrendous pain. SPD is a condition that appears in pregnancy. It causes the ligaments holding the pubic bones in place to soften, so the pubic bones move ever so slightly. Every single time I moved, especially as my baby grew, it felt like someone was sticking a hot poker deep into my vagina. The pain was so intense that it made me cry out in pain, scaring the shit out of anyone who was in my vicinity. But I kept reminding myself: *These are my decisions. I chose the business; I chose the baby.*

Cicely was born in summer 2009. The birth was easy – I have always been lucky when it comes to delivering my babies – and almost immediately the SPD symptoms less-ened, but they were to be replaced by something worse.

I didn't fully understand how mentally ill I was, but, looking at my new baby, I felt weird, off. I'd stare at her tiny, helpless body as she breastfed and I would feel dislike for her. I didn't want her near me, with her scratchy hands grabbing at my boobs. She had trouble latching on and my nipples were cracked and sore. Feeding her was a painful nightmare.

'Please stop it,' I'd whisper. 'Stop hurting me. Please latch on. Please stop it.'

These feelings became more intense, until sometimes I'd just watch Cicely crying for me and I'd do nothing.

For the first two weeks of Cicely's life, before I went back to work, I chose to blend breastfeeding and formula feeding. I told Neil it was to make things easier for him when I went back to work – and in part, it was. But it also helped me cope with my weird feelings. I hated myself for feeling this way. *You're so unbelievably shit. You don't even look after your kids full-time, and now you don't even want to feed your own child. You selfish bitch. What good are you? They'd all be better off without you.* These thoughts went round and round my head every day, overwhelming me.

Ten days after Cicely was born, a health visitor diag-nosed her as being tongue-tied. That was why she couldn't latch on and my nipples were cracked and bloody. A small procedure was booked in to fix it but it just made my low mood worse.

'How could I not know, Neil? She hasn't been feeding properly because she can't. She physically couldn't do it. And all this time I didn't know. I just thought she was being difficult. I'm so shit.' I sank deeper into episodes of self-hate as the weeks passed by. I didn't feel that I was any use to Neil, to my staff, to anyone. I felt a constant paranoia that something bad was going to happen, but I kept it to myself. I didn't want to seem weak or out of control.

'How have you been feeling in yourself, Sabrina?' the doctor asked.

'Yeah, alright, I suppose.'

She looked over at me from her computer screen, first at me and then at the sleeping baby at my feet. We were there for our three-month post-natal check.

'I see that Cicely had a procedure for tongue tie,' she said, looking between me and the screen. 'How was that for you both?'

I looked at her, then quickly down at the baby. 'I should have known she couldn't feed properly. I should have known she needed help.' My throat started to constrict, getting tighter, and I began to shake.

'Why do you feel you should have known, Sabrina? I see from the notes that it was picked up by your health visitor early – is that right?' she checked gently.

'I'm her mum, and I should have known. I thought she was being fussy. I thought she was being difficult.' The pitch of my voice rose, and tears gathered in my eyes. I mustn't cry. I mustn't cry. I continued to look down, talking hurriedly. 'I didn't like it. Her fussiness. I blamed her. The baby. I blamed her, but it's me. It's my fault. I don't know her. I don't know my baby.' I couldn't stop the tears. They fell down my cheeks, hitting my lap and dampening my trousers. 'I'm just so shit at everything.'

There was silence. Just me, and my sobs. The doctor passed me a tissue from her box and asked very slowly, 'How long have you been feeling like this?'

I looked up for the first time since I started talking. There was concern in her eyes.

'I don't know. For a while. It's been worse for the last few months.'

Silence again.

'Sabrina, have you heard of post-natal depression? I suggest that you may have been experiencing depression for some time – and we'll get to the bottom of that – but your baby's birth has been a catalyst for it getting worse. But we can support you. You'll get the support you need. Can I make some suggestions?'

I nodded.

I left the doctor's surgery with a prescription for a course of anti-depressant medication, another appointment for a week's time, details for a talk therapy group I could join, and a suggestion from the doctor to do something – anything – that got me out of the house for 'me time'.

'Have you ever tried jogging? That could be good for you,' she offered as I stood up to leave.

I'll always remember the first day I ran. I didn't want to go out running, so I kept putting it off. It had been a week since I saw the doctor. At our second appointment, she had asked me again. I lied and said I had been out running. Then I felt bad for lying when she was only trying to help me, so that evening, I promised myself that I would try.

I looked at myself in the mirror. I was carrying a few extra stone and had no exercise kit that fit me. Rummaging through my drawers, I found an old pair of tracksuit bottoms and an oversized T-shirt. 'That'll have to do,' I said, staring at myself.

As I walked down the road and under the railway bridge in an old pair of trainers, clutching a bottle of water, I was on the edge of turning back. I could see the turning for the canal towpath – the turning that signalled the start of my planned run. I stood there on the path, looking ahead and feeling scared.

'I'll do one mile. Half a mile out, half a mile back.'

That's what I said to Neil. And now that mile felt too far. I'd overestimated myself.

OK, I thought. One minute jog, one minute walk.

And I went. As I launched myself forward, my large, milky boobs almost hit my chin; I didn't own a sports bra. I could feel every single pound of my overweight body hitting the ground as I ran. Every pound of fat crushing my bones. But I carried on. And then the minute was up.

'Thank God,' I said out loud. 'How many more minutes in this mile will there be?'

Thirty minutes later, it was over: my first one-mile run was done. It took longer than I had expected – not that I had any expectations – as I had to have a long rest at the halfway point. I grabbed a metal fence at the side of the road to hold myself up. 'Just get home, Sab,' I told myself. And slowly, I did. I got myself home. I was almost on my knees as I crawled through the back door, but I did it.

'You alright, Bumble?' Neil asked with a concerned smile. 'How was it?'

I kept eye contact with him as I grabbed his hand to pull myself off the kitchen floor, my beetroot-red, sweaty face so close to his. 'It was horrendous. I'm not going to be able to move tomorrow.'

He laughed and asked me if I wanted a bath.

'Yeah. And a new body.' As I sat on my bed and took off my clothes, I realised something: I hadn't had a bad thought while I was running. I hadn't thought about much at all, actually. The only things in my mind were to keep moving forward, control my breathing and not fall over. The internal voice wasn't there, not like it normally was anyway. It was muffled by a different voice, a kind one, that whispered, 'You did it.' I felt a sense of warmth deep inside, a glint of pride. It was an unfamiliar feeling, but one I wanted – needed – to feel again.

That run was life-changing.

From that day, running became my medicine, a prescription I couldn't afford to miss taking. It provided me with a daily dose of endorphins that, when the black dog of depression was biting at my heels, kept me sane and protected my improving mental health. It was my safe space. Every single trip made me feel better – not always during the run because, at times, running felt horrendous, but always after. That feeling of accomplishment was addictive and a natural high. I craved it and became grouchy if I couldn't get it. Running was my favourite pastime, one that transformed my mental and physical state and introduced me to new friends.

But you can't outrun your demons, and I still had a long way to go on the road to recovery.

7

THIS IS THE END

It's September 2015. I'm perched on the side of our double bed in our beautiful five-bedroom house, and I have never felt more wretched. I am desolate at the thought of another day of running my business – the award-winning company I founded eleven years ago that I have willingly sacrificed so much for. I want to lace up my running shoes and sprint away from it all – away from the monster I have created.

I can't cope any more. I can't continue living this life. I feel shackled, unable to move, and I struggle to breathe through my tears. *Please don't make me do this any more.* These chains – invisible to all but me – have tightened around my neck, my ankles, my wrists. And every time I try to imagine another life, another career, they burn me, like warning shots. *You cannot change this. You chose this. There is no other way.*

People tell me I'm living the dream because, from the outside, I have everything I ever wanted. I am the boss bitch and in charge of my own destiny, aren't I?

But for me the dream has become a living nightmare. I'm trapped and it's all my own doing, because I wanted more. I wanted more respect, more money, more clients, more stuff. Material possessions that would say 'look at me, I made it'. I truly believed that once I had them, I'd finally be happy and fulfilled. I'd be able to stick two fingers up and show everyone that I'm so much more than they told me I would be.

But somewhere along the way, I lost a lot more than I gained.

And now I don't know what to do. I sit here in the dark, not knowing where to turn or who to share this feeling of dread with. Who will understand? I feel alone and so incredibly selfish. Who wouldn't want this life? Who wouldn't want all that I have? Look at my house, my car, my summer holidays.

I should be happy. But I'm not.

I can't cope any more. Being the only supply of petrol that powers this machine – the business I built of my own volition – has broken me. Sleepless nights and long days. Precious time spent away from my children. Too many missed school assemblies and plays, all because 'Mummy is working'. The only escape I can think of is to run away. I think about it all the time.

A feeling of dread stays with me all day, every day, getting worse as the day goes by. I keep a smile plastered on my face and the vomiting at bay until my staff go home. I keep 'Sabrina, Managing Director' mode turned on until I hear the door click shut behind my last staff member. This is my cue to crumble. The part of the day where I switch from boss mode to Mummy/wife mode. Slowly I push back my leather swivel chair, kick off my heels and fall into a foetal position on the floor. Making myself as small as I can, I pull my knees into my chest and cry, 'Help me, please someone help me.' I allow myself fifteen minutes like this – it's all I can afford. People need me.

As I sit here on my bed at 6 a.m., thinking about the day ahead, with the sky starting to lighten and the dawn chorus erupting, I feel like I am drowning in responsibility. I'm gasping for air.

My sobs wake Neil. 'What's wrong, Bumble?' he asks. 'Why are you crying?'

'I can't do this any more, Neil. Please don't make me do this any more.'

People deal with trauma in different ways. Some people know they have been traumatised and seek help from a doctor or therapist. They spend months or even years under the care of a qualified professional, using a combination of medication and talk therapy to understand and manage the mental health repercussions of what they have been through.

But what about the others? People who don't understand the trauma they have experienced? People who have never been told that, as a consequence of surviving their life, there will come a time to pay the piper mentally. In my experience – and the experience of others I know – if this time comes and you're not ready to address your trauma, then you find a way to trick your mind, to stop the flashbacks, to silence the voices in your head. You find a way to numb yourself, to forget.

Ever since I was a teenager, alcohol has been my friend. Alcohol has given me a way to escape, as well as confidence. It could make me the life and soul of the party or reduce me to a dribbling heap on the floor. Since having Cicely in 2009 and taking anti-depressants and using running to manage my mental health, everything had ramped up both professionally and personally. The business was booming, and I was running around in circles to keep all the plates spinning. From 2009 to 2016, everything got so much bigger. Bigger bills to pay, bigger gambles to take, more people to please. Everything, including my dependence on alcohol to cope with life, had got out of control.

The only thing not growing was my marriage. In fact, it was receding – dying, even. Our relationship was collapsing under my increasing dependence on alcohol. Neil could see what my need for 'one more drink' was doing to me – how it was changing me, the woman he loved. But I couldn't.

One night, I got so inebriated at an awards ceremony that I blacked out and threw up inside our minibus, in front of all my staff, on the way home. After another night out, I blacked out while lying on top of my young son, Brandon, and Neil had to rescue the kid, scared shitless, from under me. He saw the anxiety on our children's faces every time I picked up a glass of wine, and the impact my behaviour was having on all who loved me. But when he told me I was out of control or that I needed to rein it in, I'd fly into a rage. I'd scream, 'If you'd the life I had, you'd drink like me!' at him. I'd get mean, evil, calling him weak, less of a man. At my lowest, I told him I could do it all without him.

I knew I was hurting him, cutting him deep with my drunken words – words I wouldn't even remember in the morning, when I was full of remorse. For a few years, he forgave me and my behaviour, until one day in 2016 after a particularly drunken evening. With tears in his eyes, he gave me an ultimatum. 'If you don't get help, you need to leave our home. I can't watch you kill yourself.'

I'll never forget the haunted look on his face as he said these words.

I started using alcohol when I was fourteen as a way to check out of my life, with its backdrop of everyday racism, which led to my low self-esteem and crippling anxiety. I got drunk to manage my trauma. Back then, Broadhouse Youth Club on a Friday night was the place to be. Every fourth week was disco night, and the place would be heaving with kids from secondary schools all over the town who came together to socialise, get off with each other, drink, smoke pot and do what teenagers do. The first time I went I was shitting myself. I didn't like crowded places, I didn't like people looking at me, I didn't like drawing attention to myself. I liked staying at home because there no one could get at me – well, no one outside my family, anyway. But tonight, my two best friends Bobby and Lisa had persuaded me to come to the club, promising to 'get me off my face'.

'What the hell is that?'

'It's Martini,' said Lisa.

'What the fuck is Martini?'

'It's like a wine. My mum mixes it with lemonade.'

'Well, should we mix with lemonade?' Bobby suggested.

'Nah, fuck it. Let's just swig it.'

We discovered quite quickly that Lisa hadn't realised – when stealing the said bottle of Martini from her pub landlord parents – that it had a 'pub measure' top. This meant we couldn't just swig it from the open bottle.

'You twat, Lisa. It'll take us ages to drink this. How do we even get it open?'

It took us a good ten minutes to figure out that if one of us sat open-mouthed under the bottle while the other one pushed down the top, then we'd get our allotted mouthful. Over the next few hours, we become expert at this – and increasingly drunk.

I'd never been drunk before, but with every mouthful I swallowed I felt a sense of calmness wash over me. My heart rate slowed, and I started to feel the warm 'buzz' that my friends often talked about. It was as if someone had turned on a golden tap of relaxation juice that ignited every part of me. I suddenly felt happier in my own skin, as if I was being bathed in a warm, numbing blanket. The drunker I got, the less I cared about what people thought of me. Being this drunk gave me a confidence in myself that I had never experienced. This was the sweet escape I had been looking for all my life.

I felt like the person I had always wanted to be. I finally felt like the 'real me'. Maybe people would finally like me and accept me. I was no longer Sabrina the half-caste, NHS-spectacle-wearing, fuzzy-haired weirdo. I was like them, and I wasn't scared any more.

I never wanted this feeling to stop.

This is it. It's 2015, I'm thirty-eight, and this is the end of my life.

My naked body convulses and I'm ravaged by yet another vomit-inducing spasm. I am certain that I am going to die tonight. I have poisoned myself with alcohol. The amount I've consumed today has pushed my vital organs past the point of no return. I can't stop being sick: my body is on a mission to reject every trace of the fatal cocktail inside me.

I need to lie down, but I have to be silent so I don't wake Neil and the kids. I'm trying to trick my body into believing that all the poison is gone. I just want to sleep.

For about five minutes after each vomiting episode there is peace, and I lie on the tiled floor of our en-suite. *Why have I done this to myself again? Why do I continue to do this to myself? Why can't I stop?*

I cry silently and keep whispering, 'Please stop', but my body isn't finished yet. I'm sweating, my heart is racing, and I lurch to the toilet once again, as if getting ready to dive in. My mouth waters and the retching starts. I am the real-life version of Gollum from *Lord of the Rings*.

My convulsions have never been this bad before. I see stars as I lower myself to the floor again and rest my head on the cool tiles. I think I spotted blood in the bile I have just vomited up. There's never been blood before; that's new.

I don't want to die, but I don't want to carry on living like this either. It's not just my physical reaction that's getting worse; it seems that every sip of alcohol I take recently has a repercussion: loss of friends, severed links with family, scaring the kids.

But the oblivion that alcohol gives me is like nothing else. I love the taste of it, I love the way I relax after a few drinks, and most of all, I like people telling me that they like me better when I'm drunk. They say I'm funny. That I'm a good-time girl. Although, thinking about it, no one has said that to me for a while.

This bathroom floor situation is happening more often these days. It probably goes hand in hand with drinking more. Well, that's what my husband tells me. He says I can't be trusted with alcohol. I can't just have one drink. He says I have no self-control, that 'fun-time' Sabs left the room years ago. He says she has been replaced with someone he doesn't like, someone he doesn't want to be around.

Lately he's started looking at me in a way I hate, like I'm something alien that he can't categorise. It certainly isn't a cute or fond look. I know our relationship is changing. He says he hates me drinking and that when I drink I'm vicious and out of control. I'm not attractive. He says it's him or the alcohol. Today, just as on many other days of late, I chose alcohol. The gin bottle doesn't ask questions of me, doesn't want me to be something I'm not. Gin doesn't judge.

If I die today here on the bathroom floor, alone and naked, I'm sure people at my funeral will say they didn't know how bad it was, that I seemed to be a superwoman, and 'what about the poor children and her poor husband?' They will show sympathy; many will cry over my passing. But deep down they will know that I killed myself, with my love of alcohol and my inability to stop. I drank myself to death because I couldn't 'just have one'.

Oh fuck, the stomach ache is back again. It's building, it's coming . . .

This time the vomit tastes like metal in my mouth, metal tinged with acid. I can't muster the energy to wipe my mouth as I sink back to the floor. My heart is beating fast and strong in my ears. My breathing is shallow. *Please, God, please help me.*

'The only person who can help you is yourself.' Neil's voice is stern and loud in my ears. 'You need to drink some water.'

'I can't. It won't stay down.' I don't have any energy. I

just lie there, in the foetal position, my tears falling onto the floor. What a sight I am.

'You need help, Sabrina. You need to get help. Do you want the kids to see you like this again? Is this how you want the kids to see their mother?'

'No! But I don't know what to do. I don't know how to stop.'

'Find a way.'

The stomach ache starts again . . .

'My name is Sabrina, and I'm not sure if I'm an alcoholic. This is my first ever twelve-step recovery meeting, and I'm here because my husband has said our marriage is over if I don't get help. He thinks I'm an alcoholic. I don't know what else to say. I've been sober for three days and I feel OK. I don't know if I belong here.'

A resounding chorus of 'keep coming back' echoes around the room.

My mouth is dry and my hands are shaking. Beads of sweat make their way down my spine and soak into my skirt's waistband. I can't focus on what the person next to me is saying. I just want to get out of here. I need a drink.

The meeting closes, and I keep my head down as I don't want to make eye contact with anyone. I don't want to speak to anyone, and I certainly don't take any of the stupid fucking literature. This place is not for me. I'm not an alcoholic. It's not like I need to drink from the moment I wake up. I can go for days without drinking, actually. I just like a weekend drink and, for fuck's sake, why not? I work hard, don't I?

'Are you OK?'

I feel a hand on my arm and turn.

A small, sixty-something woman is in front of me. 'I'm Esther, and I wanted to give you this.' She takes my hand, opens it and places what looks like a bronze coin in my palm. When I look closer, it says '24 hours' in the middle.

'Each day that you're sober is a win. Each night you put your head on the pillow having not had a drink is something to be proud of. By being here you have admitted that you need help, and we're here to help you through our own lived experience. I have been where you are, Sabrina, and I'm here to say it will get better, but there will be bad days too, days when you yearn for a drink to take the edge off your feelings. But please believe me when I say that *nothing* is so bad that a drink won't make it worse. This sobriety chip will remind you of that. Keep it with you in these early days. Whenever you need to talk – whether morning, noon or night – I'm available. Here's my number.'

I've never felt so much kindness from a stranger. Tears well in my eyes. I don't want to cry, so I clench my teeth. It's like she knows what I'm thinking. With a swift manoeuvre, she hands me a tissue, pats my arm and turns to take her coffee cup to the kitchen.

I almost run from the meeting, squeezing the chip in my hand. Can I do another twenty-four hours?

'Get busy living.'

That's what someone said in the meeting.

'You wanna keep your addiction at bay? You really wanna stay off the booze? Then get busy living.'

I didn't understand what they meant at first.

'Really it means that, at those times during the day or at night when you would normally pick up a drink, you've got to find something else to do,' explained one member. 'Take up a new hobby, read a book, clean the house from top to bottom. Just get busy living. It's the times when you find yourself with idle hands that are the danger times. This is when you'll obsess over a drink. When your hands will reach for, search for, the bottle. So get busy doing something else.'

But what?

A few weeks later, an opportunity presents itself to me – a chance conversation that will change the direction of my life.

'If anyone is interested in leading a running group for women, come and talk to me,' announces Martin, the chairman of my running club. It was a cold autumn night. About thirty of us club runners – people who run with an affiliated UK Athletics running club – are huddled in the cold foyer of a sports hall, waiting to be briefed on our training session.

'Sab, you should do that. You'd be great,' insists Jenny, my group's over-enthusiastic running coach.

I laugh out loud. 'God, no. The last thing I need is to take on something else. Neil would kill me,' I reply as we venture outside to start our warm-up.

'But you've done so well with your running over the past few years, and you're *so* good with people. Just think of the other women you could inspire.'

Me? Inspire women to run? These are words that didn't sit comfortably. I'm not inspirational. I'm just a woman trying to do her best with what she has. A mum who learned to run to manage her weight, fitness and mental health. I'm no one special. There are much better qualified people than me.

But no one more qualified comes forward in the weeks that pass. After even more cajoling from Jenny, I decide to help. Little do I know that this decision – is it fate? – will change my life.

Two months later, on a freezing cold morning in January 2016, I'm standing outside our local leisure centre, feeling anxious, my imposter syndrome rearing its ugly head. The term 'all the gear and no idea' springs to mind, but I have to quickly bat it away. I can't allow negative thoughts to take over today.

Forty women have signed up to start running with me! Forty women – mostly mothers – have registered to learn to run 5K by joining my women's-only running group. I'm overwhelmed. Happy, but shitting myself at the same time.

I know that these women will feel just like I did when I started. They want to be fitter, to manage their weight, but most of all they need something to help them manage their mental health. An hour a day when they can be themselves – not Mummy, not a wife. And if running is the conduit for that, so be it.

Ten minutes to go. I pace back and forth so they can't miss me. I'm wearing a hi-vis jacket with 'run leader' emblazoned on the back and a garish bobble hat. It's important that I'm here to greet each woman, to help to quell their anxiety, to address all the fears I remember having when I joined a running club.

What if no one turns up? How stupid will you look? the devil on my shoulder whispers in my ear.

One hour later, our session is over. Twenty women are looking at me expectantly, all sweaty and red of face, their beaming smiles bouncing off me. I know that this is the start of something tremendously special.

'I really hope you've enjoyed today's session, ladies – if "enjoy" is the right word!' I say with a giggle. 'Please go home, get some water and food down you, and have a warm bath. I will email you the stretches we've just done, along with your homework for this week. It has been an absolute pleasure to spend the last hour with you.'

As they leave, they thank me for my time, my leadership and my advice. They thank me for starting this morning group that fits in with the school run. These women know that they won't be judged for being too slow, too quiet or for not looking like a runner. I know exactly how they feel.

As I sit in the coffee shop after our session, I sense a shift inside me. Yes, I feel overwhelming gratitude for the opportunity I have been given to work with these women, but this feeling is something more. It overflows inside me, filling me up with what feels like golden light. I've found something that I thought was lost forever: my true purpose.

Calmness and clarity wash over me as I realise *this* is where I'm supposed to be. This group I have created, this opportunity I have been given, is a sign from something higher telling me that I will be OK. Being ready for this moment was what it's all been about: the racial abuse, the depression, the alcoholism, my career to date – everything I have experienced has been to prepare me for this phase of my life.

To help women and anyone who feels marginalised manage their mental health through the physical act of running and to use my life experience to lead, educate and inspire – this is my purpose.

My addiction has given me this. In order to not succumb to my cravings, I had to – have to – get busy living. And I just know that this group is going to be a massive part of living without alcohol. If you believe in fate, which I do, then maybe it all started seven years ago when I did that first run. Without the doctor's suggestion to try jogging, I wouldn't be here. I wouldn't be in the right place at the right time to even hear about this opportunity.

I'm the kind of person who needs to know that I'm

making a difference. Not a difference in a financial sense, to a company's bottom line, but a difference to someone's life. If on my dying day I truly believe that I have made a difference, even to just one person, I will leave this world happy. I will have done my bit.

How long has it been since I felt I was making a difference? I know I felt like that back in 2006 when I won my first PR award, but that feeling was tinged with so much anxiety. It was based on my desire for recognition from my peers – something that I always seemed to be chasing in my professional life. But here, in this moment, that need has vanished. I know I have everything I need inside me.

It's a fucking epiphany. I can almost hear the static coursing through my veins, the excitement about my future. This lights the touch-paper for me to eventually make the biggest professional decision of my life.

8

'THE TOUGHEST FOOT RACE
ON EARTH'

In September 2016, once the 'pink fluffy cloud period' – as I've heard other people in recovery refer to it – of early sobriety had ended, the hard, emotional work of understanding why I used alcohol the way I did began. It was fucking hard going. Sometimes it felt like too much. I'd been working through the twelve-step recovery programme with a sponsor (a person who is themself in recovery and acts as a mentor to take new members through these steps) and, as I'd admitted to her, sometimes I got bored of it all – bored of talking about my childhood, my past, my life. When I got bored, I got frustrated and angry, and then all my feelings merged and I felt lost in them.

Life was fine, I guess. I wasn't hurting anyone, I wasn't getting into trouble. I wasn't really doing much of anything. I went to my recovery meetings like a good girl; I had a good sponsor and new friends who were in recovery too. But everything just felt a bit boring and flat. I felt like Bill Murray in *Groundhog Day* – same shit, different day.

One evening, as I flicked through the same old stuff on TV – *Strictly*, *X Factor*, *Who Wants to be a Millionaire?* – shows I'd normally lose myself in, I felt agitated. My sponsor said that agitation was a symptom of being 'spiritually uneasy'. No shit, Sherlock! I kept changing channel, then stopped at the sight of a man I recognised vomiting what looked like green bile into a plastic bucket. He looked in quite a bit of distress. Who was he again? I couldn't remember his name.

My question was instantly answered as the voiceover guy introduced 'James Cracknell, Olympic gold medallist, takes on the Marathon des Sables, known as the toughest foot race on Earth.' The scene cut to James hooked up to an IV in a medical tent, looking on the verge of death. This could be interesting viewing, I thought. 'Why would anyone do this?' I asked Neil, who was sitting beside me on the sofa. 'Why would anyone in their right mind put themselves through this?' We then watched footage of James training in a heat chamber at a university in Kent.

'Well, he's an Olympic athlete, isn't he? He wants to see what he can push his body to do,' came Neil's reply.

'Yeah, but he's a rower. This is running in the Sahara Desert, and he's got to run carrying everything he needs. Is that right? Like, everything – clothes, medical stuff, food, drink? Am I getting this right?'

I was almost right, as the voiceover went on to explain.

The Marathon des Sables is a 250-kilometre foot race that takes place every year in the Sahara Desert. Competitors carry all their own equipment – medical supplies, food, drink, clothes – as they make their way across the Sahara over several days, covering different terrain and distances during each stage. At night they sleep in open-sided tents with seven other participants. If at any point in the race they cannot go on, they are transported out of the desert and have to make their own way home.

'Fuck. This is brutal.' I was transfixed.

From what I could gather, every year the race includes a day and night that the competitors have to run through. This is called 'the long stage'. This stage can vary between 80 and 100 kilometres, and competitors have thirty-five hours to complete it. It's the stage at which, I gather, most participants abandon their race. To do this, they 'press the button', the button being an SOS signal which is part of the GPS satellite tracking unit pinned to them at all times. Once they have pressed this button, there's no going back. You're out.

I thought about my own running journey, from the doctor's suggestion that I try running as a way to manage my post-natal depression and the sense of achievement I felt after completing that first mile, to the way running has transformed me physically and mentally. At that point, the longest I had run was five hours on flat tarmac.

The fastest competitor in the Marathon des Sables usually completes the long stage in eight hours, the slowest in thirty-five hours. Thirty-five hours is a bloody long time. Even five hours of constant running is a long time. How must it feel to run from early morning to late afternoon, through the evening and into the next day? I couldn't fathom it. Why would you want to do that to yourself?

Fascinated, I watched the documentary as it showed footage of the highs – people finishing the race – and the lows – people's bloodied, blistered feet being treated in the makeshift medical tent aptly named 'Doc Trotters'. I was both riveted and repulsed. Before I knew it, the documentary was over and I was left with a whole host of thoughts, a weird bubble of excitement in my stomach, and one big question that I couldn't seem to shake.

Could I?

I instinctively knew that if I were to decide to take something like this on, it would be a massive commitment, the biggest physical challenge – other than childbirth – I had ever undertaken. I had to really think it over.

I was still sober – taking it *a day at a time* as I had been told to – and I did feel better sans alcohol. It wasn't easy; deciding to no longer numb yourself with your drug of choice never is, but I continued to work at my alcohol recovery programme, attending the required meetings and staying close to other sober people who were also on that path.

Neil's support of my sobriety transformed our fragile relationship for the better. I still had some way to go to earn his trust. He knew, better than even I did, what a grip my addiction had on me in the end. But from the day I admitted my powerlessness and sought help, he supported me all he could. For we were a team, something he continued to remind me of.

My children, who were then twenty, seventeen, ten and seven, all had different requirements of me and – at times – as any parent will tell you, it was overwhelming. It *is* overwhelming. But I knew that they were glad to have me there, fully present again, on call for them. They knew about my struggles with alcohol, as I'd been as honest with them as I felt able. My number one priority was to be a good mum; not perfect, but the best I could be.

I was also still running my business full-time, but I had taken my foot off the pedal a little and accepted that I needed help to keep things ticking along while I continued my recovery. I employed a few more senior people who, in turn, kept my customers happy. I was able to pay my bills, and, for me, that was enough.

So, with all that I had going on, it probably wasn't a good idea to take on the toughest foot race on Earth. Was it?

Fast forward to 13 April 2018, eighteen months since I hit the 'register' button and decided to train for the toughest foot race on Earth. Look at me now. Here I am, lying in the dark, waiting to start the day they all talk about, the one they all fear: the long stage of the race.

I wake up before everyone else in Tent 142. It's still dark

out there and I'm absolutely freezing. When I was researching what kit to bring with me, people told me that the nights in the Sahara are cold. But I severely underestimated just how cold it would be. A few days ago, I made a massive mistake by not keeping my lightweight down jacket with me. That was a massive mistake for two reasons. First, my body doesn't have the energy reserves to keep me warm at night, which means I'm not sleeping well. Second, because my body is working extra hard during the night to keep me warm, I'm using up extra energy, energy I don't have, which is impacting on how strong I feel during the day.

What I know – I have made it my mission over the past eighteen months to learn this stuff – is that from a biological point of view, the body will prioritise life-giving functions over those it sees as non-essential. So, your heart needs to beat – that's essential. You do not need to be able to run, or walk; that's non-essential. If your body exhausts its stored energy (calories) to keep your body at a certain temperature (essential), then you risk collapsing while running, due to your muscles not getting the energy they need to hold you up. I made a kit mistake that, during the long stage, I might well end up paying for.

As the sun starts to rise, the activity in camp starts to grow. Runners and Berbers walk around, the former stretching their legs and the latter readying the site for our departure. When I use the term 'walk around' to describe runners, what I really mean is 'shuffle'. There isn't a lot of walking going on; if there is, it's slow. I catch the eye of another competitor and nod good morning. He mouths it back, unable to expend the energy to speak.

There's an unmistakably weird vibe around camp this morning. Is it trepidation? Fear? If we were told we could skip this long stage – it's 86 kilometres this year – would we? It feels to me that this long stage is what everyone has been working towards. It's all people have been talking about since we got here. 'How will we cope? Shall we run in pairs or solo? How much running are we going to do? Will we have enough food?'

It's here now. Today is the day and our start time is 8 a.m.

I check my feet one more time before I put on my toe socks and trainers. I ask them to be kind to me today. To work with me, not against me. To continue carrying me forward. I look at my wide, stumpy feet, which I inherited from my dad, feet that I thought for years were ugly, but feet which – while training for this race for the past eighteen months – have never let me down. Have never blistered, rubbed or hurt me. As I rub my hard soles, I wonder whether, as I have been told so many times, my feet are indeed the way they are thanks to generations of my Black ancestors walking and running barefoot because slaves didn't have shoes in the cotton fields. This training process has taught me to love my feet, as well as my strong, thick thighs. I don't need to justify why they look the way they do to anyone. My feet work the way I need them to. They carried me here, right to this space. My thighs power me to places where others can only dream of visiting, and that's a gift.

We stand as a group of eight at the start line. Since we arrived, my tent-mates have become my family. None of us are elite; we're all competing in this race for our own personal reasons. Almost everyone in our tent runs in pairs except for me and Andy; we run solo. I like the solitude of running alone, because it means there's no pressure. No having to keep up with someone, no feeling bad if I want to slow down. No competitiveness. I can be alone with my own thoughts about what I'm doing right here, right now. I can mentally work through my own stuff without feeling the need to talk to fill the silence. Running is my therapy, and I've always preferred to do my own training and racing alone.

There's a little competitive spark between me and Andy. I can deal with that. It might even be fun to race him, to keep each other moving forward. However, we both know that this long stage is about surviving. We all just want to get back in one piece. The countdown to the start has commenced. As we hear the opening guitar chords to 'Highway to Hell', we ready ourselves for departure.

'We can do this, Tent 142!'

'Desert Feral,' came the reply. This phrase was our group's in-joke that we used as a bespoke identifier for each other while in the desert. It made sense to us, due to the feral environment we felt we were living in while in the Sahara. We were using buckets for our ablutions and our personal cleanliness standards were slipping down the list of priorities as each day passed. We really stank, but as a group we happily accepted it. We were Desert Feral.

Together we walk towards the start line. The horn sounds and we're off.

The Sahara is one of the most beautiful places I have ever had the good fortune to visit. The route of the long stage guides us through some of the most stunning scenery I have ever seen. As I pass Checkpoint Four, at about 50 kilometres, the sun is starting to go down and the temperature is beginning to cool from the 40-degree heat of the day, giving much-needed relief. I look in the direction that my fellow competitors are heading. They look like a line of tiny ants marching to the horizon. As far as my eyes can see, there are massive sand dunes bordered by jagged, imposing mountain ranges. Minutes pass as I stop and gaze in contemplation. As I do, the sky and sand turn golden. The burnt orange hue bounces off the mountains and across the terrain. It's magnificent. I refuse to move, not out of tiredness, but out of sheer wonder. I will never get this chance again.

These are scenes that, for so many years, I felt I would never see. Not because I didn't want to, oh no, but because I believed these places weren't for someone like me. Someone who was poor, someone who had never been on an aeroplane, someone who was scared to be alone for fear of being targeted for how I looked. To be here now, alone, but feeling part of something as opposed to apart, feels like medicine for my soul. I take it all in. I lap it up and then, once I feel full, I prepare to head into the second 33 kilometres of the long stage, into the darkness of the night.

'No, this can't be happening to me. Not now. Not here. I'm such a twat. Why did I forget that I would need a lighter of my own?'

I forgot to pack my lighter. Stupid. In camp at the end of each day I have borrowed a light off my tent-mates to light my stove. But they're not here for me to blag off now, are they? Because I'm solo, aren't I? A lone wolf. Nobody I recognise is anywhere to be seen. I'm sitting here with a bag of dried food, cold water, a stove and a fuel tablet. But they're no use to me without a lighter to light the stove, heat the water and rehydrate the food. *SHIT.*

I start to panic.

Words can't express how much I have been looking forward to eating this hot meal all day. There are only so many mini banana malt loaves and packets of Mini Cheddars that you can eat before they start to repulse you. I need more of an energy boost than they can give me. I *need* this sweet and sour chicken meal. I have saved this one, my favourite of all the dried meals I have taken with me, specifically for this checkpoint on this day.

I look around. There's just one other person in the tent. He's wrapped in his sleeping bag, eating slowly from a tin cup. I eye the heat that is rising from his cup. He must have a lighter on him, and I wonder if he'll let me borrow it.

I crawl over to him. 'I'm really sorry to ask, but do you have a lighter?'

He squints at me, a lack of understanding on his face.

'A lighter,' I say, mimicking lighting a cigarette.

Same look.

I point to his meal, then point to my stove. Surely he can understand?

'Non.' He looks back to his food, which is cooling by the second.

'Oh, OK,' I say, crawling back to my backpack and stove. I feel bad for even asking him, but I don't know if I can go on without getting something warm inside me. I sit for ten minutes, hugging my knees to my chest, tears stinging under my eyelids as I contemplate what I'm going to do. I need to eat. One of the mottos I have lived by in training is 'low mood, eat food'. I have found, as many other runners have, that if I don't have enough energy then my mind goes to a dark place. Low mood when running is a really good indicator that you need to eat. My engine needs to be stoked.

I spot a runner in the tent opposite me lighting her stove and, as if my arse is on fire, I jump up and head over to her. 'I'm really sorry to ask, but is there any way I can use your lighter?'

With a smile she unhooks her lighter from her bum bag and hands it to me. I have to stop myself from hugging her, and I run back to my tent to light my fuel tablet. I will eat hot food today!

WHY WON'T YOU LIGHT? Please light, please! I cannot get this fuel tablet to burn. I have placed myself in every position I can think of to shield it from the wind, but it just won't spark. I mentally reprimand myself again as I remember yet another piece of kit that I have been borrowing from my tent-mates and now do not have. Tin foil! Yes, I forgot to pack it too. This acts as a windshield for your stove, sheltering it so that you can light the fuel tablet. As each minute passes I get more annoyed and upset. I am bubbling with rage at my lack of preparation. I look over and see that the woman is packing up to leave. She glances over at me and obviously wants her lighter back. All I can do is stand and stare at the stove for a few seconds. No, it's not going to spontaneously burst into flames.

I hand back her lighter and watch her, fully fuelled by her hot meal, run off into the distance. The devil at my shoulder puts his arm around me and whispers, 'Buckle up'.

Four packets of Mini Cheddars and two banana malt loaves – that's the fuel I have to eat to get me through the rest of this stage. I don't want them. They aren't bringing me any form of joy and aren't giving me enough calories to feel anything like comfortable.

What else can I do? I have to fuel myself for the rest of this stage. I can't run on empty. I feel cold and achingly alone as I leave Checkpoint Five for the last 30 kilometres of this stage.

When I was training, people asked me whether I'd be alone at night in the desert. I didn't think I would be; I assumed there would always be someone around, whether a competitor or a marshal. But for swathes of time during this stage, I have felt completely alone out here. The only way I can tell that I am still on the route is that, every half a mile, solar lights glow green in the darkness. If it wasn't for them, I would have started to panic by now.

Why do I always choose to do these things alone? As a kid, I know why I felt the need to look after myself. It was because no one understood what it was like to be me. Not my mum. Not my white-presenting sister. Everyone who witnessed the racism I encountered showed empathy, but they didn't really get it. And because I didn't know anyone who looked like me to experience or share that stuff with, I internalised it. I knew I would have to survive it alone. I depended on myself, and my resilience, to survive.

'I do better when I'm alone,' I tell people when they offer to support me. 'I don't want to put you out. You must have better things to do.'

Up to a point these statements are true, but on a deeper level I have come to understand that it's more to do with a fear of disappointing people, of not being good enough. I wish I wasn't alone now. I wish I had someone to share this with, to pull me out of this low mood. I just can't shake it. I'm so hungry and cold.

I stop shuffling. It's been a while since I actually ran. My body feels incredibly heavy, and I'm so tired. My backpack should feel significantly lighter by now, but it feels heavier than it did on Day 1. My hunched-over posture, which I have adopted to keep myself warm, is causing my backpack to rub the skin off my shoulder blades. It stings and I can feel welts on my skin starting to rise – just like they used to when my anxiety gave me 'the itch' back in my schooldays. But if I stand up any taller the cold wind will eat away at the more exposed parts of my body and that feels worse, so I'll take the welts.

I look ahead and see that there is no end to these sand dunes. With every step I take, the sand engulfs my leg up to the shin. Taking each step is seriously sapping me of energy. Every step claims a piece of me, and I don't know how much more I can take. I'm losing energy, hope, and belief that I can do this.

'I want to go home!' I shout into the black space ahead of me.

I look down at my shoulder, where my GPS is intermittently sending its little green signal to a satellite up there. Up where, though? I look up into the black night sky. Due to the strength of my head torch, I can't see a thing, so I turn it off. It takes a few minutes for my eyes to adjust, but one by one they start to appear, like little diamonds, beacons in the sky, in their familiar patterns. The stars.

It's silent. Just me, my blinking green GPS and the night sky. I sink to my knees, take my backpack off, take a deep breath and scream. Scream and cry. Cry and scream.

I'm all alone, and I don't want to be. I don't belong here. I shouldn't be here. I should be at home in the comfort of my house, with my husband and my children. Who the hell do I think I am to be here, doing this?

I sit on that dune for what feels like an eternity, until I my voice is hoarse and I can cry no more.

'Look for the silly saucepan.' Cicely's words echo in my head as clear as day.

'Look up at the stars at night. I'll be looking there too. That way we'll be together,' I told her the night before I set off on my Saharan adventure. I look up and scan the sky for the constellation that looks like a 'silly saucepan' – our little in-joke. And there it is.

I imagine her looking out of her bedroom window up at the sky. With that thought, that connection to her, a warmth builds deep inside me. Is it the fourth pack of Mini Cheddars kicking in? Or is it something more? Her voice is flooding my thoughts – and then I remember my 'emergency' envelope.

Before I left, I asked the kids to create something for me that I could look at if I was feeling sad. They gave me folded-up pieces of A4 paper which I haven't looked at yet. I haven't needed to, but I do now. I unzip the side pocket of my backpack, turn on my head torch and gently unfold each one. Bo has drawn a picture of the whole family, the six of us, plus the cat and dog. In bold letters she has written, 'good luck, Mummy'. Cicely has drawn a picture of the Marathon des Sables finish line with a stick woman running under it.

Stick people on each side are watching her. A speech bubble with the words 'Sabrina Pace-Humphreys, Winner of MdS' features prominently.

My hands shake as I look at it. My little girl, just eight years old, believes that her mother can win this race. There's no doubt in her mind about my ability to finish. She believes I can win. It's a foregone conclusion. 'Mum has gone to win the MdS.'

I am Sabrina Pace-Humphreys. I am Rhiannon, Brandon, Bo and Cicely's mum. They believe I can do this. They believe in me. I'm going to complete this – for them. I have to. The warm sensation in my core continues to build.

I store the pictures in a pocket close to my heart and stand up. I feel better for the rest, and for remembering the true reason I'm here doing this. The kids believe in me because I have showed them that anything is possible. I have showed them how you can turn your life around, how you can smash barriers, how you can challenge stereotypes. Over the years I have worked hard to challenge perceptions of me as a mixed-race woman, as a teenage mother with no qualifications. I will continue to smash these perceptions because my kids believe in me – and as long as they have faith in me, I can do anything.

I take a step forward in the new understanding that, although I'm physically alone here, I'm never spiritually alone. I have a tribe. A tribe of my own making. A tribe of family and friends who never place restrictions on me, who don't put me down to feel better about themselves, who don't want to cage me and stop me from rising. They lift me up and remind me who I am when I forget. They are with me now, in my head and heart. We move forward together.

As I start to jog, I think back to times in my life when people have stepped forward to challenge negative perceptions – either my own or others' – of me. I remember all the times I experienced racist abuse and I endured, I grew, despite it. I remember how it felt to enter this race. For me, that meant no going back. Step by step I smashed every training goal, every negative thought, every twisted ankle, to get here.

And I remember another training motto that I have relied on when times have been hard: 'The pain is temporary, but the beauty remains.'

A motto not just for this race, but for my life.

My legacy to those who will come after me.

I say out loud to my tribe who I know are with me, 'Let's finish this.'

As I round the corner, skirting the ruins of what looks like a settlement, I see something in the distance. I know better than to trust my vision at this point in the race, and my short-sightedness is making it hard for me to focus on what I think I see ahead.

Is that it? No, it can't be. It doesn't look that far away, and I still have 5 kilometres to run.

I feel the need to recalibrate myself, so I stop in my tracks.

I look down at my running watch then back up and ahead, struggling to understand what I see.

It can't be . . . I place both hands on my forehead to shield my eyes from the glare of the sunlight. Looking down the uneven path that descends to the dried-up, rock-strewn river bed, I can't quite believe my eyes. Maybe this is a mirage? Or maybe I'm hallucinating again?

Have I done it? Is that really the finish line of the thirty-third Marathon des Sables, the 'toughest foot race on Earth', my chosen fortieth birthday gift to myself?

I rub my eyes and feel the prickle of three-day-old contact lenses awash with dirt and grime. The heat rising from the ground is distorting the view and I'm not sure I can trust my judgement. I can't allow myself to exhale and experience the joy of fulfilling what seemed at times an impossible dream.

To my left another beat-up, dehydrated, war-torn runner stops by me.

'Sweet Jesus,' he says. 'We're almost there.'

I look across at him, my comrade, my desert brother, this husk of a man who, like me, has made it this far. We're 5 kilometres from the finish. Together, in our own ways, we have fought fatigue, we have traversed this landscape on bloodied, blistered, swollen feet. We have battled dehydration, a constant energy deficit and mental exhaustion to be standing here, atop this final descent, within touching distance of the end.

I knew after 'the long stage' – that night of internal

terror – that I would get here. Today I will finish the Marathon des Sables. Now that my fellow competitor has confirmed that my eyes are not deceiving me, that it *is* the finish line in the distance, I will forever have two reasons to hold 15 April as a special date in my heart. Because today is also my oldest daughter's twenty-second birthday.

Twenty-two years ago, as an eighteen-year-old teenage mum, I promised Rhiannon that I would do everything in my power to keep her safe, to provide for her and to be the best mum I could be. Today, she will be at home celebrating her birthday – and will watch me finishing the toughest foot race on Earth. I know she'll be watching my little dot on her computer screen at home, willing me on.

'Rhiannon, my blue-eyed girl, this one is for you.'

Part of my promise to 'be the best mum I can be', I have realised in the years since, has been to show all my children that, no matter what cards we are dealt, no matter what people think of us or how many times they tell us that we can't do something, we most certainly can. I never tell my children that achieving their dreams is easy. I show them that with persistence, self-belief and a supportive tribe, we can smash through barriers.

It's time to add this accomplishment to my haul. It's mine. I start to run fast downhill, leaving the hilltop ruins behind me. I jump over boulders, dodge past rocks, kick stones out of the way. I push my weary legs as fast they will go. As I run, I remember. I remember what got me here – the journey.

From sitting on the sofa at home one Saturday night, bored and looking for something to take my mind off being sober. Finding the MdS documentary on TV and thinking 'They're all mental. There's no way I could ever do that.' I remember sitting at my computer on the day of registration, waiting for the entry page to open and paying my fee. I remember the anxiety I felt once I'd registered due to that fear of the unknown, fear of the training I would need to undertake. I remembered the conversations with Neil – and in my own head – about the sheer scale of the commitment to get to here that I would need to make.

I remember the whispered comments made by people – members of my own family and so-called friends – who believed I was 'putting training above my husband and children'. That hurt me a lot. Did people not know me at all? For a time, these comments made me question myself. But then I would step into my greatness – yes, it's a term – and remember one of the twelve-step recovery lessons I have learned: 'People's perceptions of me, which they loudly vocalise, say more about how they see themselves than they do about me.'

Ignore it and move on.

And finally, I remembered how, as a kid, I would watch those Black athletes on the telly who looked like me, winning their medals, and I would wonder how it felt. And now that was me! I was going to complete something I'd trained hard for too. Something that meant so much to me.

Today in this 45-degree heat, and with little over 3 kilometres to go, I am not stepping but running into my greatness. Everything hurts – as it should after five days of running across sand dunes, dried river beds and up and down Saharan mountain ranges – but I keep pushing forward. I look down at my watch and see that I am running at the speed I did on Day 1!

As the finish line comes closer, I think of every single person who has been part of my journey to get here. I know that they're at home, watching me on the GPS tracker, willing me over the finish line. I know they will be shedding tears, because they know what it has taken to get here.

Maybe it's the dehydration, the lack of energy, the heat, but I can almost see their smiling faces, hear their shouts of 'You got this' and 'You can do it, Sab!' I *feel* their energy cross the thousands of miles from home to here. Then I see my dog, Albi, who has been with me on every single training run. Come rain or shine, he has been at my side, keeping pace with me, listening to me as I talk to him about life, as if he is human. I look down and see him beside me, his big ears flapping in the wind as we run to the finish line together. With that, I break down. I cry. I struggle to keep moving as sobs shake my body and I gasp for air. I shout out loud, 'I'm going to do it, I'm going to complete it!' as I keep running.

When did he get there? How long has he been filming for? As I look to my side, I see a cameraman. He's filming it all: my tears, my running, my finish line moment. But I don't care. *This* is what I came for. This moment. To finish. To show them all that I can be whatever I set my mind to. To show my children that they can be whatever they set their mind to. To show anyone who has ever been told they can't, because of who they are, where they are from or the colour of their skin, that they can.

And then I see him, standing at the other side of the finish line – Patrick Bauer, the founder of the MdS. The man, the myth, the legend. Patrick started off this race thirty-three years ago by carrying all of the supplies he would need on an adventure across the Sahara Desert. The next year a few friends joined him and the race grew from there. Every morning for the past five days this man has climbed atop a Land Rover and, five minutes before the start of each day's race, has danced on the roof of said vehicle to AC/DC's epic hit 'Highway to Hell'. Passing him as I headed out for each stage, and giving him a virtual high-five, is as close as I have got up until now.

As I wait in line for my medal, I cannot control my emotions. I have finished. I have exceeded my expectations and have finished well within the top 500 competitors. I am the eleventh British woman to cross the finish line. As far as I know, I am the only British mixed-race mother of four to – in 2018 – complete the world's toughest foot race. Maybe ever. Fuck. That's me.

The enormity of what I have done feels like it could swallow me up. But I won't let it. I step forward. As Patrick places the medal around my neck, I can't stop the tears from coming. A melee of press photographers gather around me, sensing this could be a media moment, and Patrick takes my face in his hands and says, 'Bravo, Sabrina. Well done.' The cameras flash. I thank him and walk on, to be greeted by my fellow competitors who have finished ahead of me.

I pull out my last written message and hold it up to the camera that is streaming video from the finish line all around the world. My handwritten message reads, 'Happy birthday, Rhiannon'. In tears I blow her a kiss, step aside and say silently to myself, 'We did it.'

9

SNOW-BLIND

I've always worried about how to describe myself.

For so many years, until I met Fiona in that hair salon at the age of fourteen, I was referred to as – and willingly called myself – half-caste or coloured. I was OK with that, as I didn't know any different. I was unconsciously ignorant. That is, until Fiona told me it wasn't OK for people to use those words to refer to me. I was not coloured. I was not half of any caste.

Around that time, I adopted the descriptor of 'mixed-race', because that's what I was, wasn't I? Black and white. The white part wasn't my lived experience, because I have always been racialised as Black, but I always felt anxious identifying myself as Black because my skin wasn't as dark as my dad's, Fiona's or the Black people I saw on TV – my only reference points. I couldn't handle the thought of being rejected by Black people too, people I wanted to accept and like me. I didn't want dark-skinned Black people to feel I was stealing their identity, their

Blackness. So often I felt rootless, that I had no identity. Isn't ½ + ½ supposed to make a whole? I never felt that.

I grew up being told, and ultimately believing, certain statements.

You're not good enough.

You're not like us.

You're different.

When I began mountain trail running, I had to add 'Your life is not worth saving' to that collection. One summer day in 2019, I believed that I would die as a direct consequence of my Blackness. That's when I saw how unconscious – or conscious – bias plays a part in the decisions people make pertaining to preserving a person's life.

'Help me! Help me, please! I can't hold on. Please help me!' I scream, terrified.

I can't hold on much longer. I can't keep a grip of the soft, wet snow that's breaking apart in my hands. I can't get enough of a grip to pull my body – 10 stone of flesh, muscle and bone – back up onto the narrow ledge of this snowfield. Every time I try to dig my feet into the snow to get some purchase, the snow disintegrates. It's not hard enough to support me. I'm going to fall, and it's so far down. Oh my God, I'm going to fall.

I scream, as loudly as I can. 'Help me, someone, please!' With every cry, my voice becomes panicked and hoarser. 'Someone help me!'

The first man runs past me. He can see that I'm in danger, can sense my distress. But he doesn't stop, doesn't help. My legs are circling like the cartoon character Road Runner's, scrabbling to find a foothold, a stable anchor point. But there's none. It's just soft snow, crumbling off the ledge under my feet.

Another runner. Thank God. He'll stop and help me.

'Please help me, I can't get up.'

He keeps going. 'Poles,' he says, not stopping.

What does he mean? Can't he see that I can't reach my poles? They're too far away. Why won't he stop to help me?

As the third competitor runs past me, again ignoring my pleas for help, I press my forehead into the snow and cry out in frustration. I can't hold on for much longer. I'm using all my strength to hang here, on this ledge in the Alps.

I don't want to die here. Not here. Not without my family. Not alone. This is not how I want it to end. Please God, don't let me die here.

Why the fuck am I here?!

Mountain running. Two words that, for many people, don't go together. For many people just summiting a mountain is a dream – something that other people do. Fitter people, leaner people, white people.

I don't know any Black mountain runners, male or female. Growing up, no one I knew was a mountain runner or a mountain walker. I didn't know those sorts of people. I'd been taught about mountains like Everest, and I think my

Uncle Daniel had mentioned Ben Nevis to me, but that was as far as it went. Seeing people who looked like me scaling mountains just wasn't part of my lived experience.

So, what am I doing here? Standing on the start line of a mountain ultramarathon in the Alps in July?

It's a chilly summer's morning as my fellow competitors and I – there must be over two hundred of us – make our way to the start line. Some are jumping up and down on the spot to stay warm and keep their muscles loose, readying their bodies for the day ahead. According to the weather report – and I've been checking it religiously – it's due to heat up considerably as the day goes on. We might not feel it, though, because of how high up in the mountains – 2,600 metres at the highest point – we'll be running.

This time last year I was happily recovering from participating in the Marathon des Sables. Most people would have been content with that. Most people would have been happy with that. But not me. Because there's always that voice inside me that's looking for more. Always seeking to push the boundary of what's possible. Always trying to touch the limit of physical and mental endurance. Always seeking the answer to that ever-present question: Am I enough? Is this enough?

Standing on the start line next to my friend Sarah, I reflected on the challenges I have faced to get here. Just two weeks ago, while training with her, I suffered severe altitude sickness on a run. It made me slower, quieter, nauseous, but I saw it as weakness, so I internalised it. As we climbed from

Lac Combal to Col des Chavannes, the effects worsened. My nausea dissipated slightly when I stopped, but as soon as I started moving again and my heart rate went up, it came back with a vengeance. Sickness at the back of my throat, making me want to hurl.

My legs were so leaden that I was tripping on everything. And with each trip I became annoyed and frustrated. I was becoming confused too, and couldn't think straight. *How do I open this packet of food?* Weird.

'I need a minute,' I shouted as loudly as I could to Sarah. She gave me a thumbs-up from higher up the trail. I sat down, tears stinging my eyes, and looked out at the other side of the range, feeling insignificant. Has anyone else felt this way? I wondered. Although I felt horrendous, I couldn't help marvelling at the beauty of my surroundings.

You're privileged to be here. You get to do this, to experience this, when many people can't.

I gave myself a few more minutes to recover then got up and started walking. An hour later I was at the top, still suffering but knowing that the descent would – according to Sarah – bring some relief. And it did.

At the start line I felt the tight travel sickness bands on my wrist. A friend, a skier, recommended them to me. 'Worth a go, mate. They worked for me.'

'You alright, Sab?' asks Sarah. 'You've gone quiet.'

I had, but this was normal for me, especially when racing.

It's a coping mechanism and helps me conserve nervous energy. Plus, secretly, I was shitting it. *What if I get sick again? What if I need to pull out? What if I can't finish?*

'I'm fine,' I replied. 'Just want to get going.'

The race director was geeing up the crowd. I had no idea what he was saying, but as his voice got louder and louder, I knew that it was almost time to start.

'*Dix, neuf, huit, sept, six . . .*'

Here we go.

I hit my first checkpoint at just over 10 kilometres. The first few climbs and the hot sunshine confirmed how challenging the day was going to be. The terrain is rocky, and the route is often across narrow paths, some with sheer drops to one, or both, sides – paths that look barely wide enough for one person to walk safely along. Despite the heat from the sun and the nearby glistening lakes fed by ancient glaciers, some parts of the route will traverse snowfields because of how little heat reaches those parts.

I headed for the food table, which was laden with mango, oranges, sandwiches, sweets and crisps.

This is what I love about ultramarathons – runs of over 26.2 miles – the food! With each race, I experiment to see how best I can fuel my body, often with real food like sandwiches and malt loaf as opposed to high-sugar gels. Checkpoints are all I focus on when I'm running along. *How far to the next checkpoint? What food and drink will be there? Will there be somewhere to sit down?*

I refilled my water bottles and grabbed a selection of snacks to eat during the next part of my journey, enough to last until Checkpoint Two. I was eager to get on with the race and revisit that section where, just two weeks ago, I questioned my ability to continue.

Halfway into the race I had a sense of déjà vu. I looked to my right, down towards the green valley snaking its way through the mountains. I've been here before, I thought. But I couldn't be sure.

I continued running up the mountain trail. Some runners had stopped to take in the view. Reaching the top, I instantly recognised the dip of the Col and its green sloping sides. I was here – I had made it back to Col des Chavannes. I so wished Sarah was here to see how different I was this time but, due to being a faster mountain runner than me, she was well ahead of me at this point. I wished I had someone to share this moment with. I was giddy with pride. Even though I was just over halfway through the race, I had slain a demon. I knew this area. I knew what to expect from here on in. I felt confident in my ability. 'Queen of the mountain!' I felt like shouting. Yep, that's me!

Endorphins flowed through me – strong waves of adrenalin that made me feel invincible. I took some photos and a video to remember the moment. How happy I felt to be here.

'Right, let's do this,' I said to myself and started my traverse down the mountain towards the penultimate checkpoint.

*

I can't remember how it happened. I was looking where I was going, was lifting my feet up, was being careful. When we were here two weeks ago there had still been snow lying on the ground, so I had experience of navigating that. Sarah told me that by the time I returned for this race, much of the snow would be gone. She was right – a lot of it was, but a few patches remained, like the one in front of me.

I stopped just before it and looked down at my trail trainers, the same ones I'd worn two weeks ago. They had big lugs that gripped the trail. I had been safe on here, using my poles to give me stability, to dig into the snow. I only had to get through the next 100 metres of snow. *You'll be fine. You've done this before. You were fine,* I assured myself.

But twenty steps later I was far from fine. I was fucked.

It happened so fast. I was paying so much attention to what I was doing. My foot placement. My pole placement. My breathing. And then my right foot, the foot nearest the banked wall of snow, slipped from under me. Due to the camber of the narrow path, it knocked into my other foot, which gave way. Before I knew it, my lower body was hanging off the side of the path.

'Help me!' I screamed. My poles were slipping out of my hands as I scrambled for something to grab. Every move made my precarious position worse. Every move made me fall a little more. I kicked to find somewhere to anchor my feet.

'Help me! Help me, please! I can't hold on. Please help me.' I screamed louder.

Five runners passed me, all white males. None of them stopped to help me. I was clearly not worth it. With every breath I took, I was losing energy. The sheer strength needed to hold on was draining me.

'I don't want to die here,' I sobbed, pressing my forehead into the ledge.

Those five runners broke one of the moral codes of ultrarunning: 'If a person is down, if a person is in danger, you stop. You put your race to the side, and you help them. You do not leave them.'

The code didn't apply to me today. Why didn't anyone want to help me?

I'm going to die here. Die, or hurt myself so badly that my life will never be the same again. That was all I could think while I closed my eyes and waited for the inevitable to happen. 'I love you all. I'm sorry,' I whispered.

And then he appeared. The sixth man. He reached down and grabbed my forearm with his strong hand. It took me by surprise, and I shuddered because I didn't see or hear him coming. His grip was tight, like a vice on wood. He was trying to pull me towards him, to safety, but due to gravity and because so much of my body was hanging off the path, he couldn't pull me up by brute force alone.

He spoke to me in a foreign language – not French, maybe Italian. I couldn't understand him, and he knew it, so he used his body to show me what he wanted me to do. He kicked his toes into the ground, creating dents in the snow, and urged me to do the same. Still holding my forearm, he put a pole in my left hand and with his free right hand he started to ram his pole into the snow, gesturing for me to do the same. Stamping his foot and ramming his pole, stamping his foot and ramming his pole. I tried to follow his advice. *Kick your toe into the snow, dig your pole into the path. Push and pull. Push and pull.*

I was still losing my grip intermittently and, every time I did, I screamed. But his grip on my arm never waned. He never stopped urging me to push and pull myself up to the path, to him, to safety.

And then it started to work. Little by little, I gained ground. By listening to his instructions and by reaching, gripping and digging my poles into the places he pointed out to me, I got back onto the path. He got me back up there. A brown-skinned Italian man saved me. The only runner who thought I was worthy. My guardian angel.

I crawled off the path. I couldn't bring myself to stand up. My legs wouldn't have supported me anyway. I knew that I needed to get off the path, get to solid ground. He followed me closely. He had my back.

At the end of the snow patch I pulled myself up onto a boulder, turned around and looked up at him through the tears shining in my eyes. I grabbed his hand.

'Thank you. Thank you so much. Thank you for saving me. Thank you.' I knew he understood. Knew that he could see that I was totally indebted to him.

It turned out he did know some English, as once I let go of his hand, he pointed down the mountain at the tiny figures we could see in the distance.

'Bastards. Should have stopped. Bad runners. Bad for sport.'

I was crying again. 'Yes, I wish they had,' I replied. I shook his hand again and gestured for him to go. He'd done enough, and I didn't want to ruin his race more than I already had. Besides, I had to figure out what to do.

Refuge Elisabeta, the penultimate checkpoint, was 5 kilometres from where I had fallen. There, I sat on a crumbling wall and took off my backpack. I felt emotionally numb, and I didn't know how to fix it. Since setting off from where he left me, I had become more detached. I'd stopped looking around at the beautiful surroundings, stopped feeling pride in myself, stopped feeling anything.

All I could think was, *Why? Why didn't they help me? Why wasn't I worth it?*

I couldn't get it out of my head. Everything felt heavy, as I pondered these questions about the value of my life to others.

I tried to regain focus, reaching into the pocket of my backpack to pull out a piece of flapjack. 'Low mood, eat food' – that's what my coach told me. I was feeling low right now – worthless, in fact. The flapjack was hard to swallow due to the lump that was forming in my throat. I chewed once, twice, three times. I chewed for what felt like forever but, no matter how soft the food became, it felt like razor blades as it travelled down my throat. I took a gulp of water from my bottle and forced it down.

I looked around at other runners. There were just three of us here, doing what we needed to in order to regroup and continue. I looked at them intently. Each one. All athletic in physicality, not like me. All white, not like me.

And then it hit me like a hammer blow. *Was it because I'm Black?*

Realising that the runners might not have stopped to help me because of the colour of my skin floored me. I looked closer at the runners, the checkpoint support crew, the spectators. All were white and male, apart from one female volunteer.

That understanding hit me like a thunderbolt. My numbness was replaced by something else. If I had been white, would they have helped me?

Clarity. That was the replacement emotion. It was an a-ha moment, just like when you finally understand algebra or the offside rule. Once you get it, you can't understand what took you so long. You feel stupid for not seeing it.

They didn't help me because I'm not one of them. If I looked like them, like their mothers, their sisters, their daughters, they would have stopped.

In the years I have been trail running, I have normalised being the only Black person on the start line. The only Black person in the race pictures. Being different was my normal. It was the story of my life. I've internalised it because I thought there was nothing I could do to change it. I didn't know any other Black trail runners or Black mountain runners. Were there even any? Have any of them experienced what I have? Out here? On the trails?

'*Thé?*' said the female volunteer, passing me a cup.

'*Oui*,' I said. '*Merci.*' My hands shook as I cradled the sugary tea.

'You feel good?' she said.

'*Non*. Tired,' I replied.

'Ah, *oui*. But 8k to final refuge and then, *voilà*, the finish line.' A massive smile lit up her face, and she patted me on the shoulder and returned to the laden table. If only she understood what it was going to take for me to leave this checkpoint.

My thoughts turned to my kids. They're never far from my mind when I'm racing. I always think of them just ahead of me, egging me on. 'C'mon, Mum. You can do it.' Always expecting me to finish.

My babies were all I thought about while I was hanging off the ledge. I just wanted to get home to them. To see their faces. To inhale the smell of the most recent addition to my family, my first grandson, Frankie.

I need them.

What if it had been them? What if it had been one of my children, my grandchild, who had been hanging off the ledge? Holding on and begging, pleading with someone to help them? And what if, like me, it took the sixth person to stop? But what if they hadn't been strong enough? What if they couldn't hang on?

I shuddered. My numbness was quickly being replaced by something deeper, something tribal, something that stoked the fire inside me . . . anger.

I took another bite from the flapjack, a vicious animalistic bite, and this time it was easier to swallow.

I needed to get home – to safety. I needed to finish this race, not just for me, but for them. I wanted to fucking complain, to be vocal about what had happened to me. I wanted to tell the organisers so they could reprimand the runners. If they didn't know what had happened, how could they address it? How could I – we – feel safe here?

I took another bite of flapjack. The combination of sugary tea, flapjack and anger was firing me up, giving me what I needed to keep putting one foot in front of the other. I stood up quickly. 'Ouch!' My muscles had already started to tighten, due to my prolonged rest. I started to walk and the tightness eased.

I will not stop until the end. I will not stop.

10

BLACK TRAIL RUNNERS AND
THE CHARLIE RAMSAY ROUND

It took me four years to decide to finally shut down my PR business. I promised myself I wouldn't make any hasty decisions. I gave myself the gift of time, took advice, and wondered whether I should sell it, but deep down I think I always knew I wanted to wind it down. To tie up all the loose ends and go out on a professional high. That day came on 1 March 2020 – sixteen years to the day that I had launched my business, and twenty-three days before the UK entered its first COVID-19 national lockdown. That day I started the official process to shut down Trailblazer PR.

Many people who knew the old me questioned my sanity, but my mind had never been clearer. For years I had known that my PR business was no longer serving me but was, in fact, harming me and those I held dear. My gut was telling me something had to go. As I confirmed my plans to my accountant and filled out the relevant governmental forms,

I felt not one glimmer of remorse. When you know, you just know.

Since my first women's-only running group had launched in 2016, its membership had grown to over 100 women. Every time I opened registration, the group got bigger. I even had a waiting list! My women loved the community I – we – had created. Seeing them flourish was everything to me.

Following the first running session I led, I trained to become a fully qualified running coach and personal trainer. Adding to my skills bank – alongside running the business, being a mum and doing the million other things I did to 'get busy living' – didn't feel like hard work. It didn't drain me, because I loved it.

I loved being part of the twelve step recovery fellowship too. The community gave me an insight into a world that I never believed existed, a place I could live, even thrive, without alcohol. But more than that, it gave me access to a group of people who I grew to call friends, who wanted nothing other than for me to be well, and to share their life experiences with me because that helped them too. My personal running journey, combined with my joy at building my women's running community, helped my recovery because it fed into my increased feelings of positive self-worth *sans* alcohol. It was a win/win.

And that led me here – to finally having the courage and self-belief to press the submit button at the bottom of the online form that marked the final curtain call on this phase of my life. *This is it. Are you sure?* I took a deep breath, closed my eyes and pressed down hard.

I'd never been surer of anything in my life.

In other areas of my life, I didn't feel so sure of myself, and it started screwing with my head. Since my fall in the mountains in 2019, my enjoyment of trail running – still the medicine I used to manage my mental health – had taken a nosedive. Far from relieving my anxiety, at times my running fed it, leaving me feeling shaky, sick and full of self-doubt. My fall haunted every training run and influenced every decision I made when out running during that time.

Am I safe here? This question has stayed with me ever since my near-death experience in the mountains. *Would* you *help me?* the voice inside my head repeats as I pass others on my training runs. I smile at everyone I meet, to make myself seem unthreatening, a nice person, someone who deserves help. Even as I run on routes I know like the back of my hand, that fear of falling, of being left alone, has made me start to fear the outdoors, to fall out of love with trail running.

The safety of people of colour who run was brought into sharp focus for me in May 2020, when I heard about the murder, committed three months earlier, of Ahmaud Arbery, a 25-year-old Black man who, when out on a run in South Georgia, USA, was followed by three white men in their vehicles. The men proceeded to bump into him, eventually trapping Ahmaud. When he realised he was in mortal danger, he fought for his life and was fatally shot. It was reported that his murderer spat a racist slur at Ahmaud as he lay dying. The incident went viral because, seventy-four days after Ahmaud's murder, his assailants at that point still had not been detained. His Black life seemingly did not matter. Almost two years after his murder, in January 2022, Gregory McMichael, Travis McMichael and William Bryan received life sentences after being found guilty of Ahmaud's murder, aggravated assault, false imprisonment and criminal intent to commit a felony.

'We are not safe!' I cried when I saw the video. I hurt for Ahmaud, for his family, and because it took me back to the mountain and reminded me of the moment on the ledge when I had to fight for my life. But I was the lucky one. I survived.

Hearing about Ahmaud's murder in May 2020 and the fact that justice had not been served at the time hurt me and many others, especially Black runners who had experienced their own moments of feeling unsafe while running.

On 8 May 2020, on what would have been Ahmaud's twenty-sixth birthday, thousands of people from across the globe joined together to run 2.23 miles in his honour. The run was documented on social media with the hashtag #IRun-WithMaud.

When I was running my miles for him that day, I knew I needed to do something more. The run was a small thing, a marker for the pain I felt, but I didn't want this run to be the end of the uprising. As I moved forward, I thought about the act of running and how I use it as a tool to escape the trauma I have experienced. I thought about times that I had felt scared or uneasy while out running alone. I thought about the running club I was a member of, and the fact that I was one of only two Black people who regularly ran there. About how I was the only Black long-distance trail runner.

I thought back to a race in Riga, Latvia, where, while I was running a double-13.1-mile loop marathon, I was called 'nigger' by a spectator. The other white runners got cheers and applause, but I was abused because of the colour of my skin. No one I had travelled there with understood how that felt, or how it impacted my trip. All I wanted was to complete the race and get a medal like everyone else. I didn't want to be called names.

I questioned whether running was the truly inclusive space it was portrayed to be. And, finally, I wondered how many other Black and brown people who ran had experienced these things too. I couldn't be the only one. Where were they? Who did they talk to about it? Had they also asked themselves the same question: do I belong here?

I needed to find these people. But how?

Black Trail Runners

Since I'd started to trail run, which I took up when I was training for the Marathon des Sables, I could count on one hand the number of Black people I saw at events. All I saw were white faces – normally the faces of white, middle-aged men. There must be at least one other Black person here, I'd think. Maybe they're ahead of me. But if they were, I never saw them.

After my run for Ahmaud I reached out to a London-based running group leader I had been following on social media for some time. I loved their vibe and wished their group existed in my town. I emailed the founder to see if the crew ever ran on trails. If they did, I'd move heaven and earth to run with them. A few days later he replied to my message and said that, although they didn't run on trails, he had a friend who was his 'outdoors man'. He gave me his details. That's where Black Trail Runners began.

I remember my first Zoom call with Phil, the outdoors man. We went deep, quickly, as we shared our stories and discussed the issues affecting Black people when it comes to experiencing the outdoors and trail running in particular. We talked about barriers to access and how we might be able to do something to change things. We needed to take action, but first we needed to find more people like us.

Just two weeks later I had connected with five Black trail runners who also wanted to do something. The first time we met on Zoom, I remember staring in awe at the faces on my computer screen, seeing their passion for the outdoors, for running, for being in nature. These were men and women whose lived experience mirrored my own. I felt I'd come home, like I'd finally found my people. Even though I'd only spoken to them a handful of times, mainly via email, I felt an instant connection. From that first meeting, I felt we fitted together like a jigsaw, each person bringing something unique – a different perspective, skill set, personality.

'Even if this is it – just us – I can't express how happy I am to have found you all,' I said to Rachel, Phil, Sonny, Marcus, MJ and Dora. I couldn't help it. My heart and soul felt full, and I wanted each of them to know just how special this was.

In July 2020 we launched our community and campaigning group – which in 2021 became a registered charity – Black Trail Runners. We went big on our launch campaign – we needed to. We knew we'd ruffle feathers and make people feel uncomfortable, but fuck it, this needed to happen. We needed to be the driving force, to be the change we wanted to see.

In our campaign we stated very clearly that we believed trail running had a problem with diversity. We asked UK event organisers to help us address the issue in two ways: first by collecting and sharing ethnicity data; second, by engaging in meaningful, action-oriented conversations with us about the barriers we knew existed, then by making a commitment to work with us to address them.

The community grew fast. Yes, there were Black people out there – just like us – who loved trail running too. Yes, they had asked 'Where are my people?', and we welcomed them with open arms. I still get a warm fuzzy feeling inside every time I see a new member join us. I tell them, 'Welcome. You belong here.'

The campaigning and community building work demanded a lot from us co-founders, but we had committed to play our part. To do this important work. It was in doing this work, in a chance conversation with a white trail runner, that I found out about Charlie Ramsay, the Black mountain runner.

In the UK there are three classic mountain rounds (routes around mountains that vary in distance, elevation gain and number of mountain summits they include). These are the Bob Graham Round in the Lake District, the Paddy Buckley Round in Snowdonia and the Charlie Ramsay Round in the Highlands.

Until September 2020, I wasn't interested in doing any of them. They didn't have the kerb appeal I needed. Sure, every so often I was inspired by stories of runners who had completed them in super-fast times, but those people were nothing like me. Then I had a coffee with an acquaintance, a white man I met through my work with Black Trail Runners, and he told me that the namesake of the Scottish classic mountain round – the round that many people regard as the hardest of the three – was a Black man. A Scottish Black man called Charlie Ramsay.

'Charlie Ramsay is a Black man? Why didn't I know this? How have I missed this? Why isn't this more widely known?'

'You didn't know?' he said.

'I had no idea.' I was stunned. How could I not know? How had I missed this?

I spent a few days afterwards reflecting, feeling ashamed of myself, thinking about all the times when I'd wondered whether there were mountain runners who looked like me. All along there had been, and there are. I researched Charlie; I had to know more. In the 1970s he had created his round by extending an existing route. The Charlie Ramsay Round is 58 miles with 28,500 feet of ascent and includes twenty-three Munros (Scottish mountains over 3,000 feet). Charlie completed his route in under twenty-four hours on 9 July 1978, five months after I was born. Many people since have followed suit.

Even though I didn't know Charlie, I felt I'd let him down by not knowing about him. But I wasn't the only one who didn't know. All but a small number of runners I asked – and trail runners at that – didn't know that the creator of arguably the hardest UK mountain round was Black.

Why is this important? Because representation matters. Finding out that Charlie Ramsay is a Scottish Black man is a game-changer for me, a half-Scottish, mixed-race Black woman. For hundreds or even thousands of Black runners, people who have yet to come to trail running, yet to experience mountains, it's also a game-changer.

In September 2020, something else happened in my life that I never dreamed was possible. Due to the work I was doing for Black Trail Runners, I became a cover model. I – the fuzzy-haired, mixed-race kid with NHS specs – featured on the cover of the October 2020 issue of *Runners World UK*. The day it went on sale, I went to the supermarket and just stared at my picture, there on the shelf. The mixed-race woman: strong legs, strong look, good hair. I pulled my bobble hat down to my brow so no one would see my tears. My God, it was the media representation that I had craved all those years. To see someone like me . . . and it was me! I hoped just one other person would see that image and think, 'She looks like me. Maybe I can do that too.'

The headline read 'Run strong, run free', and there I was running on a trail, with a body, a skin colour, hair and nose that for years I had hated because of how different it made me from my family, my friends and the communities I inhabited. I allowed myself to feel proud, and of course I bought all the copies in the supermarket!

At our Black Trail Runners co-founders' meeting the following week, buoyed by confidence, I mooted an idea. 'I have an idea. It's big and ballsy but, if it comes together, it would be a really important step for us,' I announced to the six people staring at me through my laptop screen. 'As we know, there is a lack of representation when it comes to Black people on mountains, so why don't we put together a team of Black trail runners to take on the Charlie Ramsay Round? Imagine seeing members of our community summiting Ben Nevis together. How amazing would that be?'

Sonny smiled. 'That's a hell of a challenge, Sab. I'm not

sure that you'd get many people waiting to sign up to it. How many Black mountain runners do we have in the community? How many of them are a bit mad like you?'

'To be honest, I don't know how many people would be up for it, but I want to see. If I want to have a go, then surely other Black people will too?'

The co-founders agreed that it would be a good idea to research. I had the green light.

Months passed. Due to the popularity of the Black Trail Runners community and other more immediate projects needing attention, the challenge took a back seat. In an interview, Anna, a journalist from a media platform called The Running Channel, asked me about mountain running. Having heard me talking about Charlie on my social media platform, she asked me more about plans.

'So, Sab, when are you going to take on the Charlie Ramsay Round?'

I laughed. She had put me right on the spot. 'I want to take it on next year, but not as a solo challenge. I want to do it with a team of Black trail runners. To experience it with other people like me. To promote this round, promote diversity and stand on top of the highest mountain in the UK and say "Representation matters. We belong here."'

Anna grinned like a Cheshire cat, whooped out loud and declared her intent – the channel's intent – to support us. 'Sab, in all seriousness, if you do decide to take on the Ramsay Round, we would love to come to Scotland and film it all. This is a story that needs to be told. We'd love to help you tell it.'

My heart felt full to bursting. 'Thank you. That means a lot, and I will certainly keep you in the loop with any plans we make.'

Later that month Anna contacted me about a voiceover for a short piece of video content the channel wanted to put together about the three UK mountain rounds. The video was to discuss what the rounds were, the routes, and why the Charlie Ramsay Round was so important to me in terms of representation of Black people in the mountains. The video was shared widely on social media. Looking back, it was an important piece of the jigsaw in the Ramsay Round idea becoming a reality, as it made it possible for me to meet the woman who would be instrumental in making this dream come to life.

To get a handle on whether this challenge could, and should, go ahead I wanted to speak to Charlie. My PR experience meant I knew who to ask and how to pitch my request to get his contact details. Within a few days, I had his email address.

Charlie might not reply – after all, he didn't know me from Adam – but you don't lose anything by trying. I sent an email introducing myself and explaining the Black Trail Runners mission and my idea for the challenge. I tried to convey how passionate I was and how important it was for Black runners to know about him and the round. I pressed send. It was now in the lap of the gods.

After only a few days, Charlie got back to me. He expressed his pleasure at our mission to get onto the round, to scale summits and explore the route. It gave me the impetus I needed to take things further. I was so excited about being in contact with *the* Charlie Ramsay, and I shared my joy on social media. I couldn't believe that the man who created a UK mountain round supported what we were doing. It meant everything. But it was another message I received, from a Highlands-based female mountain guide, that laid the foundations of this challenge.

Keri Wallace founded Girls on Hills, a Highlands-based all-female trail running company. She offered to show us around the route, to help in any way she could. She had supported well-known runners and also knew Charlie. There's nothing that Keri doesn't know about these hills (that's what mountains are called in Scotland, hills!). She has been up, down and around them many times, so enlisting her help seemed like a no-brainer.

In our early calls we discussed every tiny detail of the challenge. At times I felt overwhelmed by all the logistics, but Keri's calming influence, knowledge and expertise kept me pushing forward. I firmly believe that you should play to your strengths and never be jack of all trades. Keri was the queen of the mountains: I trusted her implicitly. Once we were ready, I set about putting my team together.

*

Concentration, surprise and trepidation were written across the faces of the twelve Black Trail Runners as they listened to Keri's description of the round – the terrain, miles, ascent, ridges, summits. At the end of the session, we asked attendees to think hard about whether they could commit to the training. If they thought they could, they should contact me in two days. The months were passing quickly, so we had to move fast.

Five people contacted me within forty-eight hours: Simbarashe, Leroy, Deo, Mzukisi and Nethliee. They were of mixed abilities and none, other than Simbarashe, had significant mountain experience, but they showed an understanding of the training required to be part of the team. They, as Black people, wanted to show why representation of Black people on mountains and trails mattered.

We decided to proceed. We had our team of challengers!

Since my first email exchange with Charlie, I knew I needed to meet him. We arranged to meet at his home the day before we were due to take on the round. As I got closer to his house, I couldn't stop thinking: What if he doesn't like me? What if he doesn't want to answer my questions? What if we just don't get on?

I heard my name being called as I got out of the van. It was Anna and Tom – the film crew – who were setting up their cameras, readying themselves for the first meet.

'Are you excited? About meeting Charlie, about starting tomorrow?' Anna asked.

'If I'm honest, I'm shitting it. I just hope he likes me!'

Once they were ready, they pointed their cameras at me and I set off for the front door. My mouth was dry.

Please like me.

Two knocks.

Give the man some space. Don't overwhelm him. Read his cues.

I could see a dark shadow through the glass coming to open the door. I breathed in.

'Sabrina! Hello. You made it.' And there he was, standing in front of me. He is a stout man. Strong. Not someone I'd want to mess around with. He has bright eyes, light like mine. He reminded me of my father and my Scottish granda. 'Charlie. I'm so glad to finally meet you.'

He and his wife welcomed the three of us into their home. As Anna and Tom set up the cameras for our interview, Charlie and I chatted easily about my trip, the final preparations for the challenge, the incoming weather, and his impending trip south to visit family. Being in his presence was so easy. He felt like family.

The crew indicated they were ready to roll. For the next fifty minutes, Charlie and I talked about his training in the 1970s, what inspired him to create the round, a step-by-step recount of the day he ran it in sub-24 hours, and he gave us advice. Charlie had a way of telling stories that was utterly captivating – I could have stayed there with him, listening forever.

I kept pinching myself. *I'm here, talking to Charlie Ramsay, the Black mountain runner. He does exist. We exist!*

Alas, the time soon came for us to go and get on with the task at hand. I felt emotional as I said goodbye. Charlie was more of a hero to me now than ever. As Anna and Tom packed their camera equipment away, I grabbed him for a hug. Who knows if I'd ever get this chance again?

'Thank you. For being you.'

As he squeezed me back, he said, 'You're welcome.'

I shed happy tears because I now knew that we truly had his support. As I set off on the final leg of the journey to Fort William, I knew that I wanted to make him proud.

I'm so nervous. My anxiety is sky-high. What if something happens to one of us up there? What if one of us loses our footing and falls? What if one of us dies up there?

The drive to Fort William wasn't the calming experience I hoped it would be. Some last-minute logistical issues were stressing me out, and the rising wind and rain didn't help. If the weather worsened, we'd have to postpone the challenge.

I arrived in Fort William at dinner time, turned into the hotel car park and almost collided with Simbarashe. There he was, my teammate, in his Adidas sliders, a Morrison's shopping bag in one hand, a portion of McDonald's fries in the other. I laughed.

'It's good to see you, mate!'

As we greeted each other, some of the tension I had been holding for what felt like eternity started to release.

I sent a group message asking everyone to meet outside. Mzukisi had been delayed by work and was due to arrive later that evening, so the first to join us was Deo, an amazing, yet unassuming man, who was currently 374 days into a 381-day run for justice to end racism.

Next to join us was Nethliee, my fellow female team member. She was new to trail running, but had worked her ass off over the past few months to be as ready as she could. She was one of the most resilient, strong-minded women I've ever had the pleasure of meeting.

And then came the force of nature that is Leroy – funny, talkative but a hard-core amateur athlete. He's a self-professed nutrition freak – 'coz you can't be feeding the body with no shit, man' – and is often seen taking off his top and skanking (dancing) on trails up and down the UK. He's a true joy to be around.

It was the first time I'd met Keri from Girls on Hills in person. Keri and her team of female mountain guides would be with us, supporting us and ensuring our safety, every day of this challenge. I hugged her so hard when I saw her.

Sitting around a table with these people, I felt like I'd come home. The connection we had developed over the months was apparent to all who saw us together. We were strong. We were ready.

I'd arranged a live social media interview for 7 p.m.,

after which we agreed that we would head to our rooms and prepare our kit, bodies and minds for Day 1. During that interview we bounced off each other as we answered questions from viewers and described which aspects of the challenge we were most looking forward to – and what bits we weren't. There was so much laughter, and it felt like another release of the pressure valve that had been building for months. Viewers said that they wished they were there too – that's how strong our vibe was.

'Does anyone have a spare pair of shoes?' Mzukisi messaged the group later that night. After I'd sent a reply – 'Are you serious??' – he confessed that this was his idea of a joke! Thanks, Mzukisi. I checked my alarm and went to bed.

Day 1 was going to be a big day. We had decided to get as much of the route done as we could, so we needed to start early. We didn't know how we would work together, so we needed time to figure that out. We left at 4.30 a.m. and headed towards the village of Kinlochleven, the start of the ascent to the first Munro of the day, Binnein Mòr.

I hadn't met Mzukisi and Leroy prior to the challenge, so it was amazing to finally be in their company. They were faster runners than me but Mzukisi, being a military man, really understood the importance of being a team player. This was not about how fast we could run each day; it was about being out here together as Black people. Mzukisi was 'all for one and one for all' – throughout the challenge, he took the lead in ensuring that no one got left behind.

My fall in the Alps is always with me. When I see a mountain ridge or a narrow mountain path with a drop, the memory floods my brain. My heart beats faster, my legs go weak, I start to sweat. As we reached the start of the first out-and-back ridge (meaning you have to traverse the same ridge line twice in order to summit), I looked ahead. My heart rate increased at the sight of the sheer magnitude of it. This exposed, narrow, rocky ridge with slopes, almost vertical, that fell away a few thousand metres to the green valleys below. The sunlight that broke through the clouds illuminated our path, making the ridge look like a gleaming knife edge. Ahead I saw Leroy and Keri slowly traversing this Grade 1 scramble, as it's technically known, and I knew that if Keri in particular was taking her time, this was going to be a horrendous section for me.

'Stay low. Keep breathing. Don't panic,' I told myself as I crawled across the ridge towards our first Munro of the day.

It felt like every twist and turn of my body would make me slip. I was getting slower and becoming more panicked. *I'm supposed to be team leader. Look at me! I'm pathetic.* I didn't want to show how scared I was. 'I just need a minute to refocus,' I said to Mzukisi, who was just behind me.

'Of course, Sabrina. There's no rush. We're a team. Together. This is not a race.'

His words gave me the confidence to stop, to refocus. Keri saw I was struggling, so she let Leroy go ahead and came back to me, asking me to follow where she put her feet and hands. Her showing me the way like this reminded me of my Alpine mountain saviour. I was safe.

Touching the peak of that first Munro on Day 1 was a massive achievement for me. Standing atop the mountain together, surveying the environment in quiet contemplation, was powerful. I pivoted to take in the 360° view, and I felt a sense of awe and peace like no other I have known. 'It's so beautiful!' I said to no one and everyone. I was dumbstruck, as I often am when stopping to marvel at these environments, places that still feel so new to me, by the beauty of the Grampian mountain range. The darkness between the crags and the pure white brilliance bouncing off still snow-capped summits completely entranced me, as did the jutting skyline of these ancient mounds with lush green valleys at their feet. I could have stayed there all day just taking it in. No words were needed; it was spiritual and healing. We soaked in the moment and, once we had captured our obligatory picture, our fists in the air in celebration, we made our way back along the ridge to bag our second Munro of the day, Na Gruagaichean. Even though it was arduous, we knew once we had traversed this and the next section, we could progress forward onto a new section of the route.

Mzukisi offered to go in front of me so I could see exactly where he was putting his hands and feet. I gladly took him up on his offer. Having a fellow Black person care about me and my safety meant everything to me.

At the foot of the final climb after we bagged our third Munro – An Gearanach – and after making our way back along the iconic, but scary as hell, ridge known as Devil's Ridge, Keri saw a solitary figure standing atop our fourth Munro of Stob Coire a' Chàirn. 'That person hasn't moved in ages. They're either lost or they know us and are waiting for us.' She got her phone out and looked at the messaging app we'd been using. 'It's Nancy! And guess what, she has cakes!'

Keri's business partner had climbed up with a load of cakes in her backpack, simply because she was so eager to do all she could to support us. That's the kind of woman she is. My pace increased tenfold because I love cake! We hit the top and were greeted by Nancy's warm smile, infectious energy and welcoming patter. After crossing that ridge, I needed that care – and the sugar hit – more than anything.

After approximately twelve hours of run/walking, during which we covered 21 miles, 9,951 feet of ascent and summited eight Munros, we reached the youth hostel at Glen Nevis, the official start/finish of the Ramsay Round. Although we had started at a different spot earlier that day to allow for the bad weather, it still felt really special to finish Day 1 here.

We were knackered but elated. Tired but proud. Stronger as a team. Seeing the smiles on my teammates' faces was all I needed to know that the hard work had been worth it. We were out here, doing this – and hopefully inspiring others. That feeling will stay with me forever.

*

Multi-day challenges have pros and cons. The pro is that at the end of each day, you get to rest and recover in a hotel or a campsite. The con is that with each day, your body and mind get more fatigued and you know that more is to come. It isn't over. This knowledge is a blessing and a curse. Your fears about what the day will hold bring internal demons to life, their voices whispering 'Can you handle this today?'

Having amended our route due to the weather system, we knew that Day 2 would be an easier day. But fuck me, the climb up to the first summit didn't feel easy at all. We had five mountains to ascend, and 40 miles to go.

The weather was fine when we started. The sun was out and the sky was dotted with fluffy white clouds, but as we got higher, I grew colder. 'Can we stop so I can put another layer and a jacket on?' There were nods all around. It seemed like everyone was feeling the same but as they were all focusing on putting one foot in front of the other, no one had mentioned it.

It's the small things that catch you out. Not listening to your body when it's giving you signs that it's too cold, hot or hungry. Not paying attention to a hot spot on your foot: ignoring it until, when you finally check it, it's turned into a massive blister that feels like a hot poker every time you take a step.

We layered up and got going. Soon it got even colder and windier, and the clag – a Scottish/northern word for fog, mist or low-level cloud – started to close in.

'Can you imagine being out here on your own?' I said to Simbarashe. 'I would have no bloody idea where the summit was; I can't even get a signal on my phone. Thank God Keri knows what she's doing.' I looked further ahead and saw that Keri and her co-guide had their maps out too. We were walking into a misty abyss.

We were quarter of the way through Day 2. Although we'd come across a number of runners and walkers, they were all white. We hadn't seen any Black people. Had I expected to? No. That was why we were here, after all. To represent. Did I hope that we might? Yes. I wondered if we'd see people like us here, or whether there just wouldn't be any other Black people in this place. Like we don't exist at all.

Five hours into the day, we stopped on the banks of the River Steall. Keri had been surveying to find the shallowest point at which we could cross and ascend what looked like a vertical mountainside – an ascent that was covered in green, with no big rocks or sharp edges. I saw no discernible path up, and wondered how the hell we would climb it. But I put my trust in her that we would be able to.

The climb was nasty. I grabbed tufts of heather and moss as I crawled up the side of the mountain, face to face with the undergrowth, face-planting on occasion. When I did, I just wanted to lie there and rest, be still and succumb to whatever happened, but my bloody team wouldn't let me. It's like they knew what I was thinking.

'Come on, you Cotswold mountain goat,' said Simbarashe.

I gave him a 'don't fuck with me' smirk, which then turned into one of my signature cackles. 'My legs are too short to keep up with you, bigfoot! You just keep going with your Go-Pro and let me be.'

As each hour passed, I better understood the importance of doing this as a team, in a group with shared experiences of navigating life and dealing with challenges that only Black people could understand. This was totally new for me, as I was normally a lone wolf. Only ever rely on yourself, I used to tell myself. That's the way it has always been. But this experience was changing my mind. I was starting to see the advantages of trust, companionship and care.

'You seem quiet, mate. Are you alright?' asked Simbarashe. His question took me by surprise as I didn't think I was being quiet; I was just being me. As we hiked to the third Munro, Beinn na Lap, I pondered this out loud.

'The talkative side of me is just one aspect of who I am, Sim. I grew up so shy and introverted, and when I'm stressed or feeling low, I go back to that. It's a coping mechanism, really, to help me conserve energy for when I need it. I'm OK. And I'm comfortable enough with you all to feel I can be silent. Quiet companionship. Isn't that what it's called?'

He smiled an understanding smile, and we continued to walk. Thirty minutes later we reached the third summit of the day, Beinn na Lap. As we surveyed the next part of the route, Keri made an announcement: 'Guys, we need to have a conversation about the rest of the day. Given the pace that we're travelling, the distance left to cover and the two Munros left to climb, we will likely be out here for another six to eight hours. I'm concerned that if this is another massive day in terms of time on feet, it will seriously impact your ability to complete tomorrow's climb up Ben Nevis and the other 4,000-feet mountains. We need to make a decision on whether we start an early descent today while we can, or keep going.'

This had to be a team decision. I looked at the others. 'How do you feel about exiting today's route earlier? Tomorrow is the day that we've all said we want to complete. We've all said we want to ascend Ben Nevis and stand together as six Black trail runners at the top of the highest point in the UK. But this is not a decision I want to make alone.'

My thoughts were echoed in their responses. Within a minute, a decision had been made. Of course, we could have gone on and spent six, seven or eight more hours out there, but, as Keri said, that would have seriously impacted our ability to cope the next day. That was going to be a seminal day: as far as we were aware, there had never been six Black trail runners at the top of the UK's highest mountain. We all wanted that moment so badly. The sensible option was to exit and recover as much as possible.

It took us ninety minutes to exit the route. When we reached Corrour railway station, one of the most remote stations I'd ever been to, we were relieved. The day was done.

But there was still one challenge ahead – familiar to us, but still unexpected.

Crowding around one of the wooden tables outside the railway station café, we unstrapped our backpacks before placing our orders.

'I need to use the ladies. I'll be back in a minute.' As I walked into the café, something happened that stopped me in my tracks. A family sat on a comfy leather sofa by the fireplace, and three men sat on bar stools at the counter, and they all gave me *the look*. The stare followed by quickly looking away and dipping their heads when they remembered it was rude to stare. The look is one I have experienced – internalised – my whole life. It said to me: 'You're different. You're not like us. Why are you here?'

Their microaggressions hit me like a freight train. I hadn't been prepared for it, or for the silence that followed. It spoke a thousand words. It shouted: 'Something isn't right here; something doesn't fit – and that something is you!'

I wanted to walk forward to the toilet, but I couldn't go any further. My legs wouldn't let me. My body went into freeze mode, just like it did on the mountain ridge yesterday. I did the only thing I could, which was turn around and get out of there. Fast. To safety. To my friends.

I told my teammates what had just happened. Of course, they weren't shocked. I had been caught off guard because, for the last forty-eight hours, I had been cocooned in a bubble of safety. A bubble where I was equal. Where I didn't fear being othered or made to feel less than. Having to deal with it again unexpectedly had taken me by surprise.

Deo, Leroy and I decided to go in together. When we entered, we were met with the same response. Stares and silence. *There's more of them*, they were thinking.

We stood in the middle of the room, unable to get near the counter due to the three rangers claiming their space. Each man deciding not to move their seats the small distance to the right or left that that would have enabled us to step forward and place our order at the till. Empty seats in other parts of the small café were claimed by coats and bags, not people, and certainly not moved as a gesture of goodwill to us. Each action – or non-action – on their part I felt as a microaggression. We just stood there, as if we were on display, chatting to each other as we waited for someone – anyone – to take our order. Our voices felt magnified as we spoke about our day, about what we wanted to order. It was obvious that everyone was listening to us – the Black people – trying to understand what we were doing there.

We ordered and exited swiftly.

'Wow, man,' said Leroy as we walked back to our table. 'They acted like we were about to rob them.'

'They're not used to Black people,' said Deo. 'And that's why we're here, brother. To represent.'

As we sat around the table devouring our tea and salty chips, I felt a sense of togetherness – of safety – that had been lacking in my life. I didn't need to explain why entering the café overwhelmed me, and I wasn't accused of seeing something that wasn't there. Because the others also felt it and have lived with these microaggressions. It further confirmed why doing this challenge, in this way, with people like me, was one of the most important things I would ever do.

The first alarm went off at 3 a.m., the next at 3.10 a.m. I was so anxious about sleeping in that I decided to set two alarms, just in case.

My body hurt, a lot. Last night's recovery was poor. I had an argument with my oldest child, Rhiannon, which centred around me being overly sensitive about my children not loving or respecting me enough. It resulted in me spending a large portion of the evening – when I should have been eating, drinking or sleeping – crying my eyes out. Woe is me.

Over the years I have realised that when you are a woman like me – self-motivated, outwardly confident and perceived as *strong* – people find it hard to know how to love you the way that, deep down, you *really* need to be loved. Women like me don't often get hugs or flowers. We don't get the tender loving care we so often crave. And sometimes that stings, because we bleed too. We need to be looked after too. And by God, when we ask for that or, as I did last night, get upset when care isn't shown, people – even our own family members – don't know how to react, because that's just not how they deal with you, is it? It's not *their* job to provide that comfort, that's for us to do.

I manoeuvre my legs over the side of the bed, ball my hands into fists and gently massage my quads. I push against my thigh, like a baker kneading bread, trying to work out the tightness in my muscles. Do they feel better afterwards? Not really. I opt for a caffeine jump-start and hobble over to the kettle.

Our first climb is 4,000 feet to the summit of Ben Nevis – the longest ascent I have ever done in one go. I know it's the longest that all but one of my team has done, but we're absolutely determined to do it and to reach the summit together.

The first climb of the day is steep. Nancy tells us that this section is referred to as Heartbreak Hill and that local athletics clubs use it to practise repeats on.

'Hill repeats? Up here?' asks Nethliee. 'I'm going to struggle to get up here once.'

We all laugh. The thought of doing repeats up and down here as a training session feels crazy but Nancy tells us that's what the current record-holder of the Ramsay Round, a local doctor called Finlay Wild, does. In 2020 he set a new male record for completing the round: fourteen hours. Training on ascents and descents such as this would have gone some way to conditioning his legs for that record-breaking run. That's the thing with running on terrain like this: you only get better, stronger and faster by continually practising on it. That's why the best mountain runners live in places like this. The mountains are their playground.

They get to know the hill routes just as we get to know local road and trail routes.

As I ponder the nature of training, the weather turns. It was bright when we set off but now, as we head past a lochan on our left, the clag rolls in and the temperature falls. It's time to manage ourselves. We stop to put on extra layers and prepare for worsening conditions.

'Snow! There's snow!' shouts Mzukisi. I look ahead. At first I can't see it, but as my eyes adjust, it's as clear as day. What I thought was mist is in fact a snowfield ahead of us.

'It's almost midsummer, we're due to summit the highest mountain in the UK, and we're in snow!' I shriek.

Of course, we stop and get photos, throw some snowballs, then continue upwards. After a while I look at my watch. The ascent calculator is at 4,000 feet.

'We must be almost there,' I say to Mzukisi. 'The summit must be close.'

We hear the film crew before we see the summit. They know how much it means to us to reach this point together.

'You made it, guys,' Anna shouts. 'This is it – this is the summit.'

As we look up and to the right, we spot it: an eight-foot-tall circular structure with a narrower column in its centre – the trig point of the summit. This is the bit we need to touch, to know we've done it.

I can't believe we've reached the top together. My heart

rate is high from the climb, and now a rush of emotion is building inside me. I look across at my teammates, already making their way to the summit, and I slowly walk over to join them. This is a first. A team of six Black trail runners, together summiting the highest mountain in the UK.

Finally, after months of planning, of early morning training sessions, of testing kit, we stand at the top together. Our success, and relief, mean that tears start to fall – not just from the physical and mental toll that this challenge has taken on us, but emotion from years of being held back, pushed down, of being told that these weren't spaces for us, of being othered. We huddle together, hugging each other. Our circle of trust. Our community. So strong together.

We stay that way for a few minutes, slowly realising that our dream has become reality.

'Can you put into words how it feels to have made it here?' Anna asks as the camera rolls.

I can't. I just can't adequately or eloquently verbalise all my feelings. There are no words. I give the best answer I can and throw her question to the others. I'm too overcome with emotion for anything I say to make sense.

Johnny the photographer takes some photos and Deo pulls out his 'representation matters' banner – a visual reminder for anyone who has forgotten why we are here.

Nethliee decides that she has completed all she wants to for the day. Ben Nevis has always been her target, and her mission is complete. Simbarashe, managing an ankle injury, also decides, due to the uneven terrain ahead, to accompany Nethliee back down Ben Nevis.

'There's no point in making this ankle worse. I'm content. I'm happy with what we've done here.'

After saying goodbye to them, Mzukisi, Leroy, Deo and I start our descent to Càrn Mòr Dearg Arête and Munro number two.

No way. No fucking way am I getting over there. Not on that. Not here. Not now. I don't want to do it. I can't do it again. I look over at the ridge we have to traverse to get to the next summit.

Càrn Mòr Dearg Arête is an exposed ridge that connects the summit of Ben Nevis to the summit of Càrn Mòr. It's an epic ridgeline, 4,012 feet high, and – for any competent hill walker or runner – a great wee Grade 1 scramble.

'We're going to get some epic shots here,' says Johnny. 'All we need is for some of this clag to clear for you to really get a sense of where you are.'

I don't want more of a sense of where I am. I can see where I am. I don't want to be here. Panic is setting in again. *Holy shit. Not again.*

As my teammates start to scramble carefully over the first jagged, slippery rocks that form the apex of this ridge, I feel myself freeze. I want to move, I really do, but I can't. I can't see clearly where I should put my feet and hands to be safe, to stay on the ridge. *I don't want to die here. I don't know what to do. I don't want to do this.*

I try breathing in and out slowly to bring down my heart rate.

'I just need a minute,' I say to Ailsa, one of Keri's guides, who is shadowing me.

'Of course, Sabrina. There's no rush. Take your time.' Her voice is so calming, so gentle. It's just what I need right now.

Keri has sussed what's happening and nimbly weaves her way past the men and back to me. She looks me dead in the eye and shows me exactly where to go, talking slowly and pointing to specific places on the rocks where I should place my feet and hands. I do as she says. I follow every single instruction and, slowly – ever so slowly – I start to traverse the arête. Once I'm over the first few boulders, Keri makes her way back to the front and leaves me in Ailsa's hands.

'Sabrina, when you take hold of a rock and move, really pull into that rock,' she tells me. 'Rather than put your whole foot on a flat piece of stone, push off the edge. You'll get better grip doing that.'

These simple pieces of advice are common sense really, but in my panicked state, I need her prompts. As I keep on traversing, I start to believe in my capability to get over the ridge.

As Ailsa leads me forward, we ask each other questions about our lives and how we got here. When she says she's a mum too and had her first child at eighteen, I stop. 'No way! So did I! Look at us – teenage mums on the mountain. Boom!'

As we talk about our experiences, we bond even more. This woman gets me. She's been there, experienced the same judgement as I did.

'If only they could see us now, Sabrina. Look at us, look at you.'

I stop and look at this amazing, capable woman who is shadowing me, volunteering her time to be an ally to us and keep us safe.

'We have proved we can do hard things, Ailsa. We are fucking she-roes!'

It's the spark I need for this final bit of the ridge, to help me remember how far I've come – not just as a Black person, but as a girl that people said would never amount to much.

Looking up, I see that the summit is getting closer. The terrain is easier to navigate as we reach the peak. I'm not going to die today.

When we summit the last Munro of the Lochaber 4,000s – four mountains that are each 4,000 feet above sea level – I know I'm done. When I touch the summit, I feel an overwhelming sense of peace, of contentment and achievement. Looking at my teammates, I sense that they feel the same way too.

As we stop for some food, I share my thoughts with Keri. 'I think I'm done. I'm super happy with what I have achieved and feel that now is the right time for me to finish this final stage of the challenge.' I felt as a team we'd done what we set out to do on this three-day challenge: to traverse as much of the Ramsay Round route as a team of Black trail runners as we could and, in that, to represent for Black people in this mountain space. 'I want to sound out other members of the team, as they may want to continue, but I'd like to come out of the route at the next exit point.'

Keri says that she has been having the same conversation with the strongest member of our team, Leroy. I share with the team how I'm feeling and give them the option of continuing. Mzukisi's wise words seal the deal. 'This is a team effort – there's absolutely no benefit to our mission in pushing onwards without you. I think we've done what we set out to do, and we should finish together.'

My throat tightens. 'OK, gang. Let's make our way home. To our teammates.'

Keri estimates that we'll be walking for another two hours until we reach Simbarashe, Nethliee and the rest of our support crew at our rendezvous point. As we join the West Highland Way and walk along the bank of the River Steall to the finish, the sun shines brightly on us. It really feels like the universe is trying to burn the beauty of this place into our souls.

Our finish is Steall Falls – a waterfall famous for being in films such as Harry Potter. As we walk the final steps towards the waterfall, we can see people in bright clothing in the distance. It's our guides and film crew! Johnny the photographer – who has accompanied us on every step of this leg – runs ahead to capture the finish.

'I really hope Simbarashe and Nethliee are there too, but I can't see them,' I say to Mzukisi.

As we get nearer, we hear claps and whoops. As their faces come into sharper view, we see the joy on their faces. When we reach the waterfall, I marvel at it: it flows strongly, powerfully, down the side of the mountain. Nothing stands in its way, just like nothing stands in ours.

And then, from behind the crew, out jump Nethliee and Simbarashe. As they run towards us, Deo, Mzukisi, Leroy and I crumble. Of course, I am the first to lose it. My emotions are so powerful that I can't stand straight. I bend over, hands on my knees, as emotion rushes through me: joy, gratitude, sadness that it's all over, immense pride in what we have achieved.

Simbarashe is the first to comfort me. His caring arms envelop me in a brotherly hug. No words are needed. He knows what this means, the significance of what we have done, the importance of what we have achieved for our community.

As I stand and gather myself, I look over at Deo. Beautiful Deo, who is on the final days of his 381-day 'run for justice' streak. He is crouching, sobbing. Nethliee is comforting him, so I go to them. I put my arms around his shoulders and hold him.

'Let it out, Deo. Let it all come out.'

And he does.

Our other teammates join us and we huddle together again, the six of us, sharing this safe space. Together we stand, having completed something that many people said would be impossible.

'No one is crazy enough to join you on a challenge like that,' some said. But they did join me: not because they're crazy, but because they want to inspire, to show that we do belong here, that we can do hard things like this. We want to inspire future generations of Black children to be what they can now see. And that's why representation matters.

We stand together in the knowledge that, by sharing our journey, by being supported by white allies on this challenge who not only filmed and photographed our journey, but held our hands every step of the way, we have set a precedent. We have shown how to realise a dream – with hard work, commitment and courage. We have shown that Black people can do this.

That's activism at work right there. That's the power of representation. Because together we are stronger. Together we can make change. Together we can inspire. And together, as a Black community, we can continue to claim our rightful place in spaces such as this.

Lying in bed after the challenge, the voice of my old dance teacher Fran comes into my head.

Stand tall and be proud.

She said these words to her dance team – led by me, a Black girl – as we prepared to start our dance, to lead the fete queen and princesses. I'll never know if Fran knew the impact of her decision to put me up front that day, of giving me that gift, but her words have stayed with me always, and today they are louder than ever.

Stand tall and be proud.

And I hope I have made her proud, that mixed-race girl in the blue skirt and white polo shirt with ribbons around her wrists. I hope that she's pleased with the life I have led, the chances I have taken and the decisions I have made on this journey. I hope that, if we met now, she would be inspired, that she wouldn't feel so alone, that she'd know she'd be OK. I hope that I'd be someone that she'd want to spend time with, to learn from, someone who would make her feel good about herself – just like Aunty Fi.

I try hard to nurture that girl in all I do: to be what she needed to see. To stand tall and be proud. It's now my job, my soul's purpose, to embody this in all that I do. I want to make her proud. All the lessons I have learned – and continue to learn – I want to pass to the next generation. Why? Because I now have grandchildren. I have been blessed with three grandsons and, since their births, I have a renewed sense of purpose, a bigger fire in my belly. I have a duty of care to them. If I can play a small part in changing their world for the better, then I will continue to do this to my dying day.

I don't need a crown to be a queen. I am exactly where I am meant to be, and where I want to be.

I never want this feeling to end.

EPILOGUE:
THE TROUBLE
WITH RURAL RACISM

I've seen the words 'race war' used time and time again in the media since June 2020, since George Floyd's murder, and since Black people worldwide came together to protest about their treatment and vociferously demand change.

The murders of two African American men – George Floyd and Ahmaud Arbery – are just two crimes against Black people that I have discussed in this book – murders which impacted upon me greatly and changed the course of my life.

But, for those of us who feel compelled to stand up and talk about our lived experiences and our intention to work to change the narrative, overt physical, verbal racism and microaggressions happen almost daily.

We are the everyday casualties of this fight for equality. I won't refer to it as a race war. It's not. The casualties include relationship breakdowns that emanate from uncomfortable conversations about racial injustice and one side feeling attacked. They include a person's mental health taking a nosedive after being called 'woke', 'snowflake' or a liar\one too many times, even though this is your lived experience, your life.

These everyday casualties may seem insignificant, but each small casualty of this fight adds up to something bigger, something uglier, something more dangerous. The resulting behaviour – the post-traumatic stress – may take months, even years, to show itself, but I guarantee you, it will.

In my opinion the events that I and other Black people experience emanate from a lack of empathy, a total ignorance of atrocities committed against people who are not white, and – worst of all – silent approval of the inequality against and mistreatment of people based on the colour of their skin. Unfortunately for me and for other Black and brown people living in rural towns, this inequality and mistreatment is commonplace. We face it in the street, we are targeted online, and some of those who are elected to serve us – people in positions of power – show us how little they care for our lived experience by responding to our stories of trauma with racist tropes.

One of my own casualties was the ending of a friendship with someone I considered one of my best friends. This casualty was insignificant to everyone else, but it still hurts me, and always will. Over the years, we shared many friendship-deepening experiences: relationship break-ups, addiction, bereavement. Each year our relationship got stronger, until June 2020, until I stood up to the racism I had experienced in this town. Her town.

I noted my friend's non-attendance at any of the town's Black Lives Matter protests, but I didn't give it too much thought at the time. I was consumed by just getting through it, a day at a time. Her lack of messages wasn't unusual – after all, she had a lot on her plate with a new baby and a new house to take care of. I understood.

Well, I thought I did. We were both under pressure. Not only had my profile increased as 'that woman who stood up and claimed that the town was racist', but something else had happened that was taking up my attention and my energy.

A local councillor had responded on social media to the town's Black Lives Matter protest – and the video of me speaking, in particular – with a tweet stating that 'All Lives Matter'. She had also shared and commented on other racist online content, seemingly agreeing with some high-profile right-wing commentators. The story exploded locally and I – along with other Black community members and white allies – was actively gathering support from local constituents who believed that the councillor should be officially held to account for her actions.

One night, after a particularly difficult day, I posted some links on social media to anti-racist material and urged my friends who had been silent on the subject so far to come forward, to support me, to help achieve change. And, oh boy, did my friend come forward! She hit me with both barrels. According to her, my promotion of Black Lives Matter during a national pandemic was irresponsible. I was in no position to call out people who chose to stay silent for fear of backlash, and she would not be lectured or dictated to by someone like me. The icing on the cake? She would not play any part in my 'witch hunt'.

When I asked her for clarification about who I was supposedly witch hunting, she made it clear that she believed I was unjustly targeting the poor councillor. My friend was more concerned about this woman – a stranger she had no relationship with – losing her job than she was about the hurt I was feeling.

The poor councillor? It took a moment for my brain to engage and understand that she meant the woman whom we were trying to hold to account for sharing racist content online. I was taken aback. This was the first time that my friend had communicated with me since I stood up at the BLM protest, and rather than speak to me one-to-one, she chose to go for me as a response to me asking for help. That cut me deep. So, I did what I thought was best; I took the conversation offline so that it was between just us. I needed to really understand what the hell was going on.

In that call she made it very clear to me that she didn't agree with my activism around 'this BLM stuff'. She questioned me about why I had been silent about this for so many years, in the time that that she had known me, and, in an accusatory manner, asked: 'Why now?'

'I don't know why I've never spoken to you about it. For so many years I just tried to bury it, tried to work hard to be someone that was known for other things, things that people would like me for, things that didn't bring into account the colour of my skin. Because I just wanted people to like me.'

Her tone changed as she tried to placate me, saying that people did like me. That my colour had nothing to do with it. And then that line was uttered, that fucking phrase that people feel they can say to people like me, people of colour, in order to make them feel better.

'I see you. I don't see your colour.'

And there you have it. The get-out-of-jail-free card for people who don't want to admit that maybe, just maybe, they need to address their subconscious and conscious bias on race and the inequality that persists for people of colour. By saying, maybe believing, that you don't see colour you are shutting yourself off from understanding the plight, the injustices, the systemic racism that people who are 'of colour' face. Your white skin tone dictates that you have the privilege to 'not see colour'. How lucky you are. I used to wish I were you.

'But being black, being mixed race, being different to most people who live here has had negative repercussions for me and other people like me. Whether you claim to see colour or not, people of colour who live here have and are being treated badly because of the colour of their skin. Me, your best friend, has and is still being targeted, and rather than support me, you choose to go for me. I ask my friends to speak up, to help me in the work to tackle racism in this town and you do, BUT you accuse me of inciting a witch hunt?'

And with that she switched back to defending the councillor. Back to worrying about this woman – this stranger – losing her job.

'But it wasn't just one comment, was it? This was not a one off, a momentary lapse, there have been more. Tell me, do you believe that people who are elected to serve us, the community, must show leadership when it comes to issues of discrimination, racial equality and fairness?'

She didn't like that, her tone flipping again. She retaliated and said we were baying for blood, that we were inciting hatred. That we wanted to ruin the poor woman.

'I'll tell you what I want. I want people like her to be held accountable for their actions. I want other councillors to know, with no question of a doubt, that sharing content that can be classified as racist is not OK. That if they do there will be serious repercussions. This is not a witch hunt; this is us saying that this is wrong. That this is not appropriate behaviour, and we will challenge you on it.'

Her silence on the other end of the phone was difficult to

decipher. Did she agree? Did she still think I was leading a witch hunt? Had I given her food for thought? Our conversation ended when I heard her child cry in the background.

'Go back to the baby. We'll speak more another day.'

And with that the call ended.

A few days later, our friendship ended fairly abruptly when I received a screen shot of a racist post in which a white man who lives in our town sarcastically apologised for being white, for being afforded his middle-class upbringing, apologising for feeling the need to apologise. Many locals had replied to this post with negative statements about their 'woke' friends, dismissing the 'lies' about racism occurring in the town and, of course, sprinkled between these were the 'if you don't like it here live somewhere else' comments.

And then there was hers. Comments along the lines of me – her friend – becoming obsessed with Black Lives Matter, not wanting to hear other people's opinion and being all-consumed by it. There was that punch in the stomach again. As I subconsciously held my breath, I read the comments in response to hers. Comments that called me 'selfish, worthless, not worth the time of day'; the same comments that I had heard for so many years when I was being bullied or told not to make a fuss about what I was experiencing.

I sent her a screen shot of the message stream. No words. Just the images.

Her response? She asked if I was stalking her now.

That was the last communication I had with her. The same day, she blocked me from all her social media. I had been erased. My apparent obsession over amplifying the struggle of Black and brown people in rural towns was something she had chosen not to hear. It didn't fit with her own beliefs; with the press of a button, I was gone.

It's so easy to filter people out and create a personal echo chamber to include only voices and organisations that share your views. Hell, social media platforms set up algorithms to show us more of what they believe we want to see, thus reinforcing our beliefs, but I don't want to see what a computer, or some social media person in Silicon Valley, feels I should see. I want to be challenged. I want to engage in conversation on topics that matter, topics on which disempowered voices need to be – must be – heard. I want to help to create change. That means continuing to amplify my voice, continuing to engage in difficult conversations, continuing to do small things each day. All these things, when put together, lead to big change. If that means I'm obsessed, then so be it.

As soon as I stepped up and made that speech at my town's Black Lives Matter protest, I knew I wanted to work to improve the lives of Black and brown people in rural towns – and to take this further, to the trail running community. I want to see change there too, to encourage more Black people to start trail running and enable more diversification in this outdoor space. I am definitely obsessed with playing my part – no matter how hard it may be – to make long-lasting change.

It doesn't come easy. My short time as an activist has been a rollercoaster. It's a continual learning curve, but it's a ride which I am firmly strapped into. People from all walks of life ask me, almost daily, 'What can I do to help?' My first response is to direct people to resources that contain exhaustive lists of material that can be read, listened to and watched. There's so much information out there, and knowing where to start may be confusing, but that's part of the work we should all be doing against racism: doing our research, consuming information, asking questions of ourselves and others. I cannot – we cannot – do the work on everyone's behalf.

In my short time as an activist, I have been asked to recount my personal experiences of rural racism so that – mainly white – people can 'really understand how bad it is for people like me living in rural towns'. Often it seems that, if these people can't see me figuratively bleed my trauma out by telling them what has happened, it's somehow not real. Why? Because my experiences and the experiences of others seem so 'out of character for this town' to them. Prove it – prove it happened! That's one of the reasons I wanted to write this book: to tell my story and show what my experience of growing up and living in a rural community was, and is, like.

I think a lot about how racism in rural communities can be tackled, and have been actively involved in groups in my own town that have been tasked with looking at this topic: racism that has been endured for years 'under the radar' by rural Black and brown people, and therefore not addressed by national, city-centric policies and initiatives.

How can we start to eradicate rural racism on both a personal and professional level? I am not an academic. I am a person of colour who has spent forty years living in a rural town. I'm suggesting the steps below as a framework we can use to start to address the issues faced by people like me who want – and need – to see change.

1. Admit and accept

I've learned that when people feel threatened or fearful, their first response is denial. When it comes to racism in the countryside, locals and those in charge of government purse strings don't want to accept that rural racism exists. To admit that their beautiful, sleepy towns and villages harbour a dark underbelly means taking the shine off them. When associated with racism, a Britain in Bloom town can fast become a 'Britain in Doom' town. This tarnish could ultimately affect their tourism and wealthy city-dweller second-home economy, which rural towns up and down the country rely on. So, denial is their first form of defence.

I saw that, first-hand, in June 2020. Sheer incredulity by locals who absolutely believe that 'racism doesn't happen here', that we are trying to stir up race problems where they don't exist – problems that should be the concerns of other towns, other cities, other countries. This town, they say time and time again, welcomes all!

In seeking to diminish or deny the lived experience of people of colour in rural environments and insinuating that they are merely 'jumping on the bandwagon' is to tell them that they don't matter. It's subterfuge. A tactic to silence us.

Until you – as a person, an organisation or a politician – take the time to listen to people of colour living in your town, you cannot and will not see the everyday racism that occurs on your doorstep. Only by consciously putting to one side all that you feel is right about the place in which you live, and by opening yourself up to the possibility that there are racial injustices happening right under your nose, can you start to address rural racism.

You must take the leap from ignorance to acceptance and admit that there is a problem. Only then can you embark on the path to change.

2. Inventory of self, businesses, organisations

It's January 2021. As I sit here writing this chapter, we are deep into the United Kingdom's second official COVID-19 lockdown. We moved into our new home two weeks ago.

There are boxes everywhere but, rather than unpack all the boxes and place the same items in the same places they were in our previous home, I'm doing an inventory. Every item I take out of a box, I'm asking, 'Do I need this?', 'Is this functional?', 'Have I used it in the last twelve months?' If I can't answer yes to all three questions, then the item goes to charity, to be recycled, or the bin.

This inventory is for items in my house but I believe it can work for individuals, businesses and organisations that serve the rural community and want to eliminate rural racism. An inventory can help those who want to make change assess where they are now and work out what needs to be kept, changed or discarded to address rural racism. Why? Because how can you know what needs to be addressed within yourself or the organisation that you represent if you don't take time to properly understand the current state of play? A question you could bear in mind throughout the audit could be as simple as: 'Does this work towards the goal of eliminating rural racism?'

If you belong to an organisation, public or private, look at your human resources department, your senior management team, your policies, customer services, products and services. Work the inventory a department at a time if that feels more manageable, but do the work. Until you fully understand where you currently are, how can you seek to make a start on facilitating change?

I have had to do this work too. I always will. I have

unconscious and conscious biases, just like everyone else. Growing up in a white town, being told things about your race time and time again, seeps into your psyche. I have had to perform several inventories on myself. It's been incredibly hard, but self-development doesn't come easy. For anyone looking to perform their own personal inventories, I would urge you to use, as a guide, one of the many respected workbooks out there (see the References).

3. Representation

People of colour don't feel represented in rural settings. We especially don't feel represented in rural government settings. We are not heard, understood or supported. For example, there are thirty-three councillors in my district. One is a brown woman, but the rest are mostly white men, and a few women. This scenario is replicated in rural councils across the country, and I believe it feeds into the lack of initiatives for Black and brown people living in rural towns.

I always wanted to live in a city simply because I knew there would be more people there who looked like me. When I visited London as a kid, every other person on the street was Black or brown. I'd see politicians such as Diane Abbott on the telly and wish that they fought for a local initiative or better equality for me, here in my town. I'd hear about Black music artists who sang or played music on the streets, and

I'd want to live that experience. In rural settings, people of colour don't encounter any of those things. People of colour are often forgotten about.

Due to more Black and brown people living in cities, these communities are at least considered when decisions are made on policy, resourcing and community engagement programmes. For all my life, it has felt that I am not considered. I am not represented. It's no wonder my sense of identity was lost for so many years; I had no one to model myself on. I had no people of colour as my peers, my teachers or leaders, so I internalised that there must be a reason for this. We're not good enough.

Let's look at local government. How do you encourage more Black and brown people into roles that will shape initiatives and policies that have local impact? You start at grassroots level. You take the time to find ways to effectively communicate with Black and brown residents, you give them a platform, you work to upskill and develop them. You take their hand and show them the way. And the more Black and brown community leaders you engage with to facilitate this, the better.

Since June 2020 I have been approached several times about running as a councillor. My first question was 'What does a councillor do?', then 'Is it a full-time job?' and 'What's the pay?' These are questions you'd ask about any job you wanted. To have more representation where it matters in order to make real change, organisations such as rural councils need to demystify the application process, clarify the scope of the role and describe how working as a councillor can help to shape initiatives and policies that will be of direct benefit and relevance to Black and brown people living in the community.

Without attention being paid to greater representation across private, government and associated agency roles – police, social work, education – Black people will always be under-represented and will never experience parity. We need more Black representation in positions of influence and power, and we need support to help Black people get there.

4. A seat at the table

How can you begin to tackle rural racism if you don't consult and include people of colour as part of the decision-making process?

A few months ago, people of colour in my town were referred to as an 'agenda point' in a local government meeting. An agenda point! We weren't allowed to join the full meeting, but had to wait to be invited in. I now understand that this is a norm for UK council meetings but, due to our lived experience, lives spent not feeling seen or heard especially by those in local power, to be treated like this felt to me like a sucker punch, another microaggression. When we were allowed in, we were given time to state our case and were then politely removed. Did we feel better after the meeting? No. Did we feel that we were treated as a box-ticking exercise? Yes. Has anything that we discussed been further explored or implemented by the council? No. Had we been a part of the decision-making process, not an 'agenda point', do we feel we could have made a difference? A resounding yes.

When it comes to making decisions that affect local policy, resourcing and initiatives, we demand a seat at the table. When an organisation asks how they can make change, my first questions are: 'How many members of your workforce are Black and brown? How many members of your senior management team, the people who are responsible for making decisions, are Black or brown?' These questions are often met with an uncomfortable silence, fidgeting and beard scratching (because there's often a noticeable lack of women present too). You cannot make decisions on how to tackle an issue as important as rural racism without members of the Black and brown communities being part of the process, making these decisions with you.

Due to the high percentage of white people in positions of power in the UK, decisions are often taken on policy, funding and resourcing without asking for real input from Black rural community members about what we really need or will respond to. As I said before, due to a lack of representation within these agencies, our voices aren't heard, and decisions are taken that do not serve us.

5. Community groups

As a kid I never had anyone – a parent, teacher or youth worker – offer to help me develop relationships with other people of colour in my town or county. I felt totally and utterly alone. An alien. I remember the first time I saw someone who wasn't white – someone mixed-race like me. I was at a county schools sports day and she was taking part in one of the races. I remember watching her intently from afar, a bubble of excitement bursting inside me. I could see that her skin was like mine, her hair was like mine. *She was half-caste too!* I needed to find out her name and what school she went to. If I knew her, she might want to be my friend.

I was nine years old, and I yearned to connect with people who looked like me and lived like me. Maybe if she lived here too, there were others. Other people like me who experienced what I did. But there seemed to be no way for me to connect with them. Black and brown people living in rural communities still don't have adequate access to community groups solely for people of colour. There are few youth clubs or initiatives to bring us together and help us share our experiences. If we want to engage with other people of colour, we must instigate that contact ourselves, often via social media. There is no central support, no resource apportioned to help us.

How does an organisation start to address this important need? You must cast your net wide within the rural community. Engage with educational facilities, doctors, social workers, youth workers and – if you don't already know them – with those already working with the community.

Look at city-based initiatives that cater for diverse communities. Take the time to research groups that are in place to bring together people of colour, groups that tackle issues of race that Black and brown people understand and live with daily.

Over the past year three UK groups – Black Trail Runners, Black Girls Hike and Flock Together – have been set up to provide active communities for Black and brown people to enjoy the countryside, while also providing a safe space where they can share their lived experiences. With greater support, these volunteer-led groups could cast their net wider. For people living in the countryside, I see encouraging and supporting groups like this as an easy win. We need more safe rural spaces where we can heal.

6. Education

My primary and secondary education included being taught about local people of note. Local white people. At no point in the 80s or 90s was I taught about Black history. At no point was I taught about the slavers who used the money they made from their sugar plantations to build local railway lines and country estates, or how the arch just up the road from me was erected in celebration of the abolition of slavery – the only such monument to be built in the UK.

At no point did any teacher, or any curriculum, state that we should be taught Black history. Everything I learned, I learned from books that I chose to read, the television, and Fiona the hairdresser.

The lack of curricular resources when it comes to the teaching of Black history, especially local Black history, colonialism and its past and present impact on local diverse communities in rural education settings continues to this day. In June 2020, the statue of notorious slaver Edward Colston, was pulled down and dumped in Bristol harbour. Images of Colston's graffitied bronze monument being pulled through the city's streets were beamed across the globe. This act, which took place during the city's Black Lives Matter protest, ignited passion on both sides. It started debates across the world on the need for statues, what they signify, what we learn from them, and – for statues that depict men and women who made their money from the exploitation, enslavement, rape and murder of Black people – whether as a society we need to pull them all down.

Seeing that statue of Colston being pulled down, dragged through Bristol's streets and dumped in the harbour was momentous, and something I am glad I witnessed. I learned more about local Black history in a few hours than I did in the twelve years I spent at school. When that statue was pulled down, millions of people across the world learned about Colston, his slaving, the money he made, and the Black people who died at the hands of his company – millions more people than would ever have walked past his statue in Bristol, something I had done many times.

Currently, a Black woman who lives in my town is talking to local schools about their curriculums and sharing resources on how to add depth to lesson planning when it comes to Black history. She's a midwife and is doing this while juggling her career, kids and home life. She's doing it because it's important. But why should she have to take this on?

We have challenged our local council on the curriculum in rural schools. The feedback we have received is that it's 'not their domain', since the county-based local education authority (LEA) is responsible for education. But, when we questioned the LEA, it said that they are led by national policy – Whitehall policy.

Some – not all – inner city schools do cater for the Black and brown communities they serve. So, if their curriculum can make room for Black history, why can't this be filtered down to rural schools? If we are to develop fully rounded future generations, we cannot continue to pick and choose which elements of history are taught to suit an old-school narrative. It's a recipe for ignorance – and, when it comes to racism, it's a dangerous precedent to continue to adhere to.

LEAs serving rural locations need to address this

urgently, because the future lies with our children and our grandchildren. To ensure that real change happens, and to work to develop future generations who are anti-racist, the government – and organisations in charge of rolling out policy – must realise the importance of including Black history in primary and secondary schools. This should happen through the core curriculum and extracurricular activities. Education providers must open the hearts and minds of children to different cultures, ethnicities and religions. There's so much that rural schools could do to foster a more inclusive approach. When it comes to education, and broadening minds, one size does not fit all.

7. It's never too late to admit you got it wrong

When you've toed a party line – whether personal or professional – for as long as you can remember, changing your stance is hard. People don't like to have their beliefs challenged and, even when every piece of evidence points to their opinion being fundamentally wrong, they will stick to it and defend it. Why? Because their moral code has been built on these beliefs; everything they feel to be right or wrong is shaped by them. So, if they are flawed, then what? Maybe they'll need to look back at their lives and perform a full inventory of every decision they've made. For some, that's too much to contemplate. They will never publicly say 'I got it wrong.'

But challenging these beliefs, the views you've formed on your own due to your lived experience, is part of the self-development work that we all need to do. Admitting that maybe you got something wrong is one of the biggest declarations a person can make when it comes to fighting racism. That bold admission is the first step in the process of doing the inner work that will lead to personal, local and global change. It always starts with individuals.

When you admit you got it wrong, there will be someone out there who will want to help you get it right. They will have already started doing their own work to challenge their racist beliefs and will want to share what they have learned.

I lost a close friend because she couldn't admit that she got it wrong. This personal casualty shows what can happen when people are unwilling to change. Relationships break down, people are erased, and conversations stop. The cycle of racism continues.

8. Continue to do the work

It never ends. The work to address racial inequality generally, and rural racism specifically, never ends. You may sigh when you read this. You may say to yourself, 'I don't think I have the energy or the time', or 'I don't think I need to do this.' But remember that small steps lead to massive change, and with each small step you take, no matter how insignificant it may seem, you are facilitating change.

You can have a positive impact on the lives of Black and brown people in your rural community. You can make this happen. You can help to eradicate rural racism.

RESOURCES

Websites

Black Trail Runners – www.blacktrailrunners.run
All The Elements – a community working to increase diversity in the outdoors. The website contains an exhaustive list of resources and a directory of its community members. www.alltheelements.co

Challenges

The Ramsay Round – www.ramsaysround.co.uk
Marathon des Sables – www.marathondessables.com/en

Podcasts

The Checkpoint – https://podcasts.apple.com/gb/podcast/the-checkpoint/id1530677708

Video

Representation Matters: Taking on the Ramsay Round
www.youtube.com/watch?v=AxxPw2UZ29U

Social Media

Instagram: *sabrunsmiles*
Instagram: *blacktrailrunners*
Facebook: Search '*Black Trail Runners*'
Twitter: *RunnersBlack*

ACKNOWLEDGEMENTS

Firstly, my family. Neil, my rock, my north star, my safe space. Thank you for loving me and being my chief crew.

Rhiannon, Brandon, Bo and CC, I love you with every fibre of my being and am so proud of all of you. I promise, one day, to stop talking about MdS!

Frankie, Teddy and Remi, to be your granny is a blessing. I promise to always give you sweets and be your safe space.

Mum, thank you for breaking the mould, and for your unwavering support through the years.

Sharon, my little sister, thank you for being you. I'll always be there for you. The same applies to Rob, Kyle, Destiny and Tyler.

To my dad, I know I can be vacant and unreachable, but I love you and always will. Zac, love you, bro. And to Pete, Julia, Carrie, Des – thanks for Neil and for your support.

To my Scottish clan, my heart is forever with you all.

There's will never be a better meal than fruit pudding and my gran's home-made chips. If you know, you know.

To Caroline Sanderson, for all those coffees and for gently pushing me to commit my story to paper. Words cannot express my gratitude for your guidance, friendship and belief in me.

To Sarah Such at Sarah Such Literary Agency, thank you for believing in me, my story and for representing me. You are the best and I am so glad to have you in my corner.

To my publisher, Jane Sturrock at Quercus, thank you for taking a chance on me as a new writer, for taking time to understand my story and for being there on Zoom when the trauma of re-living my experiences felt overwhelming.

To Alison MacDonald, my editor, thank you for all you have done to help me craft this memoir. I am so proud of it and, without your guidance and patience, it wouldn't be what it is.

And to the rest of the team at Quercus who have made this book possible, thank you.

To Sonny, Rachel, Phil, Simbarashe, Marcus, MJ and Dora. We've come a long way since that first Black Trail Runners Zoom call. To be part of this journey with you, in our various guises, working on our mission to diversify trail running, is a gift from God. Thank you for walking this path with me.

And to the Black Trail Runners' community in the UK and beyond, never stop inspiring others by being you. You continue to give me purpose. We belong here!

To Lucy, Ange, Ali and Sarah, thank you for showing me the power of female friendship. And to all the women whom I have had the pleasure to coach, you are strong, you are inspirational and remember, 'hills are mounds of opportunity'.

To Damian Hall, for always calling me 'champ' and for your support of all I do – and for one day in the future, coaching me to complete the Ultra Trail du Mont Blanc.

To John, for your coaching, friendship and honesty.

To inov-8, especially Ali and Adrian, for helping to represent me and Black Trail Runners in the early days, and for supporting the Ramsay Round film.

Thanks also to all at The Running Channel, especially Anna, Tom and Andy for their commitment to documenting our challenge. And special thanks to Keri, Nancy and all the Girls on Hills team, we couldn't have done it without you. Also, to Johny Cook for expert camera skills. And to you, Charlie Ramsay. For the man that you are, for creating the Ramsay round and for your support of us taking on your round.

And, finally, to Simbarashe, Mzukisi, Nethliee, Deo and Leroy – thank you for being the best teammates a woman could ask for and for helping me turn my Ramsay Round dream into reality. You can't be what you can't see but I, and millions of others, see you.

Representation matters; it always has and it always will.